Social Media
for
WRITERS

Imagine That!
STUDIOS

www.teemorris.com
www.pjballantine.com

Catch *The Shared Desk* live at
http://twitch.tv/theteemonster

DEDICATION

To content creators of all genres,
of all backgrounds,
everywhere.

If you walk away from this book with a new idea
for your social media strategy,
mission accomplished.

ACKNOWLEDGEMENTS

Social media has made an astounding impact on our lives, and we are reminded of this every day through Likes, retweets, Follows and Subs, and voicemail we receive from the platforms covered in this book. The inspiration behind this guide comes from the many questions we have received at conventions, at workshops, and even over a cup of coffee (or tea, in Pip's case). A huge thank you to Chuck Wendig for our kick-ass Foreword, Candy Cane Studios for the spiffy-new cover, and to Writers Digest for putting together the original *Social Media for Writers*. This Second Edition not only covers the changes in platforms well known, but introduces other online points-of-contact you may have been curious about. It was a real joy to return to this title, not only to share how much we have learned since the First Edition but offer you the writer (artist, musician, or whatever creative endeavor you pursue) new and exciting opportunities for creating communities around their works.

TABLE OF CONTENTS

INTRODUCTION 1

I: WORDPRESS................................... 9

II: TUMBLR 30

III: FACEBOOK 46

IV: TWITTER....................................62

V: INSTAGRAM.................................83

VI: PINTEREST 105

VII: PODCASTING............................... 121

VIII: STREAMING............................... 137

IX: ADDITIONAL OPTIONS.............................. 154

X: CONTENT MARKETING.............................. 166

XI: BEST PRACTICES IN SOCIAL MEDIA 174

XII: SOCIAL MEDIA SECURITY 195

FOREWORD

You're a writer over here. And over there is the wide world of social media. You've got your Faceyspaces, your Circlesquares, your Tinders, your Grindrs, your Blinders, your SexyPalFinders, your Bloobs and Gloobs and Innertubes. The point is, you've got this world out there. This connected world. This web of bridging threads that connects you, me, our phones, our computers, and probably soon enough, our refrigerators. It moves fast. The ground shifts under our feet daily.

On the one hand, social media is easy, right?

Get on it. Say hello. Say other stuff. Squawk into the void to see who's listening. (Spoiler warning: My refrigerator is listening, and my refrigerator would very much like you to go pick up a six pack of beer. Dogfish 90-minute IPA, please.)

But then, what about that other side of it? The writerly side. The authorial side. I'm a writer. So are you, I'm guessing. And you're wondering, how do I bridge those things? How do you tie together you as a writer and you as a person on the social media thingies? Is there value for you as a writer? Is there danger and peril for you as a writer? "Yes" to the first, and "Oh hell yes" to the latter.

Can you tell stories on Twitter? (Yes.) Can you find audience on social media? (Sure.) Can you burn your audience on the Internet? (Most definitely.) Can you sell books this way? (Yes, to a point, but please don't get spammy.) Do you have to sell books online and be all Author Person? (Nope.)

But how? How do you accomplish all of this? How do you keep up with what works and what doesn't? Don't different networks and services offer different... well, networks and services? A value add here, a subtractive function there?

You need help.

And so, I've written this book . . . *is handed a note* Ah. Okay. Sorry. Turns out, I did . . . *not* write this book? I didn't. Okay. Sorry. I write *a lot* of books and it all kind of blurs together.

I did not write this book.

Which is probably a good thing.

Because you need not just one Sherpa to lead you up this mountain of authorial social media enlightenment. You need, in fact, two. And so, I give you: Philippa "Pip" Ballantine and Tee Morris. They are going to hold your hand and take you on a tour of all of the weird- ness and wonder that social media has to offer—and they're also going to helpfully point out the pitfalls, too.

Because boy howdy, are there pitfalls.

You wanna do this I am an author on social media thing right? Then you need their help. You need this book. Though, before you read any further, I'll offer my one piece of social media advice. Take it or leave it— hug it close like a dear friend, or discard it like an old sock. That advice is: No matter what network you use, no matter whom you talk to, no matter the blog or the service or the size of your audience, be the best version of yourself online. Don't be somebody else. Don't be a sales machine. Don't be an asshole. Be a fountain, not a drain. Be you, with all the best stuff dialed up to 11, and all the worst stuff shoved under the bed so that nobody can see it.

So endeth the lesson.

Now: Reach out and take Tee's and Pip's hands. It's time to take a walk. It's time to take the tour. It's time to buy the ticket and take the ride.

See you online.

Chuck Wendig
Author, Blogger, General Wiseass

INTRODUCTION

WELCOME TO YOUR SOCIAL MEDIA SURVIVAL GUIDE

So what's your platform?"

This has become a common question that agents and editors often ask writers—be they beginners or best-selling authors. Once upon a time—let's say back in 2007, several generations ago in Internet time—social media was considered a distraction to up-and-coming writers and a fad to established wordsmiths.

It didn't take long for that attitude to change. Dramatically.

The beautiful thing about social media is that it's easy to pick up. It's designed in such a way that anybody can set up an account and get started. The problem, however, is that writers and social media suffer a disconnect. That is, plenty of writers hate the notion of promoting their work. They simply don't want to be that snake oil–selling writer, constantly promoting and constantly trying to hard sell their titles. And while those writers who still believe it is "someone else's job" to promote their book, the reason authors self-promote is a simple one: If you do not talk about your book, no one else will.

What complicates writers, social media, and the relationship between the two is what happens when self-proclaimed introverts pick up a megaphone and blindly go about promoting into a void. As you might imagine, things can, and do, go horribly wrong.

That's where we come in.

Throughout this book you will find nuggets of information and helpful tips on getting the most out of the various platforms covered in this book. Our "Bookmarks" point to links to check out, quick tips to employ, pitfalls to avoid, and reliable third-party expansions—like apps for mobile phones and plug-in's for blog engines. Keep an eye out for them.

We set out to write this book because we know lots of authors struggle with social media networks, platform management, and building a public image using social media in ways that make them look like a rank amateur. You may read some of what we offer in this book and think, Oh, come on, that is common sense! but some of that common sense, sadly, isn't as common as you would imagine. If you are new to publishing, one thing you learn is how agents and publishers value a social media presence. If you are new to social media, it can be daunting how many platforms are out there. This book has one goal: Show you the basics and strategies with a variety of platforms. How you build your presence from here is up to you.

All this sounds very exciting, but right about now you might be wondering who this mystical "we" behind this book is. Who is leading you into this promised land of blog posts, podcasts, and status updates?

Together we are Pip Ballantine and Tee Morris, writers of the award-winning *Ministry of Peculiar Occurrences* steampunk series. Between the two of us, we offer more than two decades of experience as professional authors, published both independently and by New York publishers. In addition, Tee offers his experience as a social media professional, having worked in corporate, government, and nonprofit positions, including serving as Chief of Communications on President Barack Obama's Open Source initiative, Code.gov. He also literally wrote the book—or in this case, *books*—on social media, such as *Podcasting for Dummies* (all editions), *Twitch for Dummies, Discord for Dummies,* and *All a Twitter.* Pip carries the distinction of being New Zealand's first podcasting author and has spoken on social media matters for authors both in her native country and the United States. She remains the only winner of New Zealand's prestigious Sir Julius Vogel award for a podcast. This is who we are, and where we began our social media journeys—in 2005–2006, on the cutting edge.

Considering we predate the hipsters by at least a decade, you might accurately say that we are social media pioneers. (And Tee was drinking Dogfish Head beer before it was cool, you young, bearded whippersnappers.)

We maintain blogs, produce podcasts, host streams, and work all the social media you will find here. Ours is a view from the trenches, and the strategies we offer for your consideration have won us critical acclaim and a variety of awards and accolades. What we hope you take away from this book is a strategy and an understanding of social media.

Social media began innocently enough as a way for authors to extend their reach to readers and other writers, and to connect on either a professional or personal level. It allowed authors to encourage others to write or offered readers a peek behind the curtain at the creative process. This online outreach evolved into an essential part of a writer's life. Today, marketing via social media channels has become a necessary part of the author's skillset as much as research, writing, and editing. However, as marketing and public relations is far removed from the creative process in a writer's eyes, social media strategies are not given enough time and attention. When moved to the backburner, mistakes are made that damage the book's audience and, possibly, the author's reputation. Most of these mishaps can be easily avoided. Others are stranger than fiction, but worth remembering and learning from.

Tapping into the potential of social media begins with understanding how all the tweets, updates, and posts began, and how authors should take the online environment seriously and maximize the tools available to them.

Book Marketing 101 (or Good Luck, You're on Your Own!)

One of the biggest myths people have about signing a book contract with a major publisher is that all you will need to do is write and everything else is someone else's job.

Not quite.

Editing and layout, most of the time, is handled by your publisher; but marketing usually falls on the author's "To Do" list. Occasionally publishers will spend some of the marketing dollars on new authors, but the majority of it is set aside for the major players: Patterson, Rowling, King, Steele. You know, the writers who don't need marketing.

Trying to understand how marketing resources are distributed in larger print houses can be best described with a quote from Shakespeare: "That way madness lies." No, it does not make sense; and as it is Lovecraftian insanity best avoided, this means you need to take control of your own marketing and promotion. No one else is going to care quite as much about your book's success as you do. This does not mean you turn down assistance from your publisher if it is offered, but marketing is no longer someone else's job. It's part of your writing career.

And believe it or not, it's not as hard as you think.

Find out when your book is scheduled for release. When you have a release date for your book, immediately go to a calendar and highlight that date. Then look at the month before and the month after. These two months are what we call your "full court press" months for promotion. That's when you're going to want to focus your content on promotion. Too early, and people will forget it by the time the book is available. Too long after the release, and people will get quickly bored with your platforms. It is possible to over-promote a title, so keep that in mind when you are planning out your heaviest promotions.

Begin building your social media channels, if you have none, or rejuvenating ones that are quiet, months ahead of your book launch. A social media plan doesn't just happen with the wave of a hand and snap of the fingers. You need to start talking, start sharing. What you put out there does not always have to be about your book—it can be about you, the writer. What are you reading? How's your editing going? Blog posts, podcasts, and updates that relate to you, your writing, and related subjects are of great interest to your community. Remember, social media is not about endless promotion. Social media is about creating connections.

Have a plan for social media and your book. Now that you're building a network, start developing a strategy for your developing platform.

When preparing blog posts, what are the topics you want to cover?

What content is most relevant to your audience? Links on fashion? Steampunk? Science? Consider what topics you believe are most relevant to what you write.

What blogs would be most interested in working with you in either tours, syndication of content, or guest posts? What about Facebook and Twitter parties? (We will get to these topics in Chapters 3 and 4.)

Asking these kinds of questions helps you develop a plan around your book, making social media your outlet to reach out to your readers and fans.

Stay within your budget. When you start receiving your advance, consider the words award-winning author Robert J. Sawyer extended to his fellow authors: "Your advance is your marketing budget." This is where you're going to get funding for services like Mention or Sprout Social and giveaway items for your social media platform (a few of which we cover later in the book).

A quick and easy—but not good—way to build your community quickly is to purchase Follows, Likes, Retweets, and Reposts through various third-party services. While doing so is a tempting way to build your numbers, it is never a good idea. Many of the "purchased followers" are nothing more than automated accounts that post nonsense (called bots), links to malicious or inappropriate sites, and other accounts that lead back to malware (applications that allow hackers full access to your networking platforms or even your computer). Also, with purchased interactions like this, your statistics are misleading. On the surface, you will have impressive numbers, but as these purchased follows are not genuine connections, your community will offer little to no engagement or interaction. While you do want the numbers, quality in your community is much more important than quantity.

When developing a social media plan, it can be very helpful to talk to authors you meet at book events and conventions. Ask what platforms work best for them, what advantages and disadvantages they find, and how they manage their writing time versus time spent marketing through social media.

If authors you speak with talk about book signings and convention appearances as the best way to connect with readers, be gracious and give them your time. Then consider this next section a reality check from us.

That Was Then: How Promotion Has Changed

Before assuming we don't like live appearances, that could not be further from the truth. We love attending book events, festivals, conventions, and book signings. We really do. They are a great chance to personally meet and shake the hands of people that are either new readers or long-time fans of our work. They are also great places to meet and network with our fellow authors—after all, writing can feel very solitary and isolating. So yeah, we love in-person appearances.

In-person appearances, however, should not be your entire marketing strategy.

First off, consider the cost of your trip. Is this a local visit, or are you traveling out of town? Second, will the two hours of sitting in a bookstore, hopefully signing books, be worth your time? What about an entire weekend at an event speaking on panels? Then there is the cost of the trip itself. Are you being compensated for anything beyond the cost of admission to the event, if you are even being compensated for that. Calculate your trip out there, food, and lodging, and personal appearances become expensive.

And now, a word on swag. If you are not familiar with the term, swag is what you are giving away for free at some of these in-person appearances. The most common examples of swag include:

- Business Cards
- Bookmarks
- Postcards
- Tee-shirts
- Coffee mugs
- Free books

However, some swag includes USB sticks with samples of your works, penlights that double as styluses, cable managers, and temperature-controlled tumblers. Promotional gear can get crazy. We have seen authors invest thousands of dollars into their swag which is impressive...until you hear about readers who take an event's "welcome bag" and draw conclusions about the authors based on the quality of their swag. (No kidding. We've seen this first-hand.) If you're curious about the fate of some giveaway swags:

- *Business Cards, Bookmarks, Postcards* — trashed, in most cases
- *Tee-shirts* — if they don't fit, they get thrown onto the event's freebie table. If they go unclaimed, they will get trashed. (If you're lucky, they might get donated to a thrift store.)
- *Pens* — Cheap pens (i.e. disposable pens) are trashed.
- *USB sticks* — Many times, these are wiped and reused for personal use.

Swag can be an expensive and ruthless game, and you run a risk of readers getting to know you for "giving away the best swag" instead of being good storytellers.

Again, personal appearances are not bad, but should not be your only strategy.

This Is Now: The Wonderful World of Content Marketing

Many authors think of marketing as this overarching need to "push your brand" because it is all about you. To a degree, yes. Marketing is about trumpeting your horn and talking about your worlds, words, and works. A very traditional approach. With social media, however, this kind of repetitive message gets old very quickly. Think about it: if, every time, you met with an author online they were talking about their books and that was all they talked about, how engaging would you find those conversations? In social media, this is referred to as Signal-to-Noise Ratio, the quality of what your statuses and updates are to your audience. If you are constantly advertising or promoting something in your feed, your audience may tune out your updates as noise. In doing so, they may miss postings that they genuinely care about or can interact with—referred to as a signal. Successful content marketing, an effective strategy that is built around social media, is all about the strength of your signal.

If you provide your readers and fans with quality content, turning your various platforms into reliable resources for fantastic media, you will establish a connection between you, your audience, and your work by sharing websites, blog posts, and other media that is not yours but related to, in some way, your worlds. This is how you begin to build a reputation with other readers, book bloggers, and authors. An example of content marketing in action can be seen in our various Ministry of Peculiar Occurrences platforms. For every post we offer that directly talks about our books, we offer five really cool steampunk posts from blogs, podcasts, and websites other than our own. Sometimes it will be the post about our book that will garner traffic. Other times, it will be a post from elsewhere on the Internet that catches the eye. It may seem unusual to offer resources other than our own on our series' channels.

You may find yourself asking us, "Why are we offering these other resources time on our platform? Shouldn't we be marketing our books?"

Yes, the end result of marketing is promoting and selling of our books; but by offering your platforms to others in your community (in the example of the Ministry of Peculiar Occurrences, it's the steampunk and science fiction communities), you reach your audience, as well as the audience of your guest contributors. What matters the most with content marketing is the quality of your content: Does it resonate with your audience, and does it establish you as a reliable resource in your genre? By making your social media channels a soundboard for topics of interest, visitors to your site may want to know more about your work. Content marketing is promotion by example, and by establishing yourself as a solid resource, you can easily reach your readers. We go into a deeper dive into the mechanics of content marketing in Chapter 10.

What You Need to Make This Book Work

"I really don't have the time for this."

This is probably the biggest excuse we hear from authors on why they are not giving social media a fair shot. Where is this coming from? Could it be the productivity lost when weeding through the variety of Friend Requests on Twitter, trying to figure out which profiles are truly legitimate people and how many are simply spammers? Is it the several hundred invitations to the latest and greatest Facebook groups that you have to ignore? Or how about on the blog you recently launched—is there a topic you feel compelled to write, and an hour later you are still working on that post? Whether it is approving others to follow you on Instagram or finding yourself drawn into a thread on Tumblr, the perceived investment of time in social media appears to be a common barrier.

Most authors know enough about social media to be dangerous, while others tend to have the wrong idea on how to manage it. What you need to make this book valuable, and to make social media work for you, is an open mind, time, and patience. Instead of tackling all of these platforms at once, select three and start developing your strategy. The magic will not happen overnight—hence your need for time and patience.

We want this book to be your trusted guide in navigating through the various online platforms out there, and we want it to help you discover the best practices and strategies for you as well as how to make them work. We're here to help you, the writer, build a community around your readers and titles.

So let's begin.

I: WORDPRESS

BUILDING AND DEVELOPING A BLOG

When you look at social media, the endgame of all your strategies is to give people one place to find you online. This is your headquarters. This is Command Central. If people want the last word on what you think, what you are up to, and where you will be signing books next, your blog should be the place where all your social media platforms lead to. From here you build a network, refine your voice, and (with the right plug-in's) sell autographed copies of your books. The blog is the nerve center of your social media strategy.

A blog can also be one of the most challenging platforms for a writer to take on.

One appeal of working with a blog is in how easy it is to update. Instead of the laborious process behind updating and refreshing the look or content of a static HTML website, a blog updates instantaneously when new content is added through a *GUI* (pronounced "gooey" and standing for *Graphic User Interface*). These updates go live once you click a "Publish" or "Update" option. Instead of having to worry about how an update will affect the overall look of the page, the blog's template you are using makes everything fit.

Blogs also offer their hosts the ability to notify their audiences of changes. Visitors to your blog are given the option to subscribe to your blog through an RSS reader like *CommaFeed* (http://commafeed.com) or *Flipboard* (http://flipboard.com). Much like subscribing to a magazine, RSS delivers new content to readers' desktops, laptops, and portable media devices. The traffic is still counted and tracked, and your readership is kept informed while your site stays current and relevant.

Blogging allows visitors the chance to interact with the blog's author, topic by topic, via the Comments usually found at the bottom of any blogpost you make live. Comments are open invitations to both guests and subscribers, unless moderated by its hosts. Moderation is best employed not only to ward off spammers, but also helps "keep the peace" if the conversation gets too spirited. Blogs also offer the option to syndicate content by posting it on other blogs, thereby increasing traffic for both the host blog and blogs referencing the original content. Concepts, ideas, and resources previously confined to a single location can now be distributed through the blogosphere.

Blogging also keeps you writing, and that is a very good thing. To make blogging happen, you need a blog engine (a GUI) that has been built for creating, posting, and managing content; and that blog engine should be WordPress.

Why WordPress?

A variety of blog engines can easily get you blogging in minutes. Just to name a few, you could use:

- LiveJournal
- Medium
- MovableType

Each of these services goes about providing you your own personal blog in its own way. Our choice option, *WordPress* (http://wordpress.com or http://wordpress.org), offers expendability in ways that other blog engines do not. First, there are a wide variety of themes to choose from. A theme is a skin that defines all the design and layout for your blog. Lots of them have the ability to do some customization, but you are ultimately limited to what the creator allows you to do. Developed by users for other users, many of these themes are free and easy to implement into your own blog. You can also find custom-built themes—for a price—that will ensure your blog is a one-of-a-kind place. WordPress has earned a solid reputation within the blogosphere as a reliable and easy-to-implement platform for all of your blogging needs.

The difference between WordPress dot-com and WordPress dot-org is expandability. WordPress.com is a fully contained package, offering a lot of plug-ins and options for free. However, you get more in the way of storage and options if you upgrade to WordPress' Premium services. WordPress.org offers thousands upon thousands of themes and impressive plug-ins, all designed and developed by WordPress users, that allow you to go beyond the basics. The trade-off with dot-ORG is that you download the WordPress software, install it, maintain it, and back up your blog on your own.

First step with WordPress, assuming you are completely new to blogging, is setting up an account. For this exercise we are starting from ground zero and using Wordpress.com to set yourself up online.

STEP 1   Go to WordPress.com and click on the "Get Started" option in the upper-right corner.

STEP 2   As seen in Figure 1-1, use the following to set up a WordPress account:
- Valid Email
- An original username
- An easy-to-remember password

You can also create an account using your Google or your Apple account.

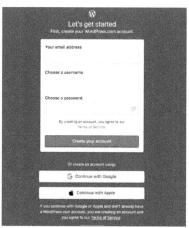

Figure 1-1: Before you get underway with blogging, you will need to set up a WordPress account. You can either create new credentials or use pre-existing ones from other accounts.

When coming up with a password, you want to come up with something easy to remember but tricky to figure out so no one can hack into your account. A mix of letters, numbers, and characters are always good, and passphrases are a heightened level of security. For example, instead of a jumbled remix of "writer" like "Wr!t3r" for your password, you could use "!am@ wr1t3rfromRichmond" making it memorable but difficult to crack.

STEP 3   Enter the domain you want for your WordPress site. For now, select the free option offered here.

The domain you would enter here would be how you want to launch your site. You can be clever about it and call your blog something like "morningwordherding" or "RVAromancewriter" or keep the branding on point and make your pen name your domain. As we are going with the free option, [your domain]. wordpress.com will be your domain.

STEP 4   Click the "Start with a free site" option at the top center of the page.

When you are wanting your domain to go from teemorris. wordpress.com to teemorris.com, you will want to return to these options and make an investment. You can review options in your Dashboard (explained below) by going to Manage > Domains in the sidebar menu.

WordPress is pretty awesome as it immediately gives you a "Honey Do" list for you and your blog. All these items are to help you come up with a great-looking blog. And this is where you get to make WordPress your own. We're going to check off some of these items and build an online HQ for your writing.

Currently, you are looking at your *Dashboard*. This is Mission Control where you can check on the statistics of your blog, modify or completely refresh the look of your blog, and manage posts and pages you create. While our account is live, we still have to build our blog, so let's start ticking off items off that "To-Do" list.

Building the Welcome Page

WordPress has worked very hard to not be "just a blog" anymore, but a fully-thought out design tool to help you build a website worth visiting. We start with working on a Welcome page.

What you will notice as we work through the various *Pages* (and eventually posts) are the different *content blocks* that comprise a Page or post. Content blocks can be more than just text. Content blocks include:

- Email links
- Embedded social media
- Headers
- Social media links

If you need something specific for your blog, chances are there is a content block already waiting for you to make that happen.

STEP 1   Click the "Update Homepage" button.

You are given a quick rundown of blocks and how they work. We're going to take a more detailed look at that here.

STEP 2   Go up to where you see the "Home" title and single-click it. Change "Home" to "Welcome" and then single-click the "Update" button at the upper-right of your browser.

The "Update" button is the "Save" function. If you want to make sure changes you make do not disappear in cases of a crash or problems with WordPress, "Update" should preserve any changes you make.

STEP 3   Click anywhere inside the "Welcome to your new site" title and come up with a greeting for your site.

Pictured in Figure 1-2, your greeting can be simple and standard ("Welcome to the Official Website of Tee Morris") or something fun ("Hey, you found me!"), but make it a welcome that represents you best.

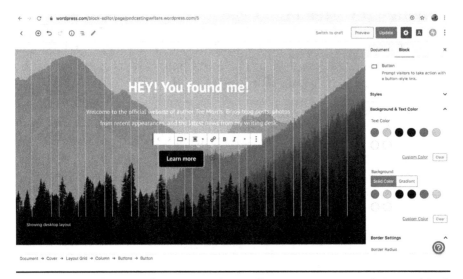

Figure 1-2: Clicking inside an area of text allows you to access that text block for editing.

STEP 4   Click inside the "Welcome to your new site!" message and rewrite it to be a message you would like to share with your audience.

If you want to learn beyond this book about WordPress from those who created it, visit http://learn.wordpress.com/ for additional tricks.

STEP 5   Click inside the "Learn More" button. The Block Options appears.

STEP 6   Click on the More Options tool (three vertical dots, located on the far-right of the Block Options) and select "Remove Block" from the drop menu.

STEP 7   In the upper-right corner of your browser window, you should see an "Update" button. Single-click that to update your Welcome Page.

STEP 8   In the upper-left corner of your browser window, you should see an arrow pointing left. Rolling your cursor over it, you should see a "View Pages" hint appear. Single-click that to return to your Dashboard.

Congratulations! You have just created a Page with WordPress. Unlike a blog post where you compose, edit, and publish your thoughts, a Page (yep, with a capital P) is static information that can be edited whenever a change happens but no notification via RSS is sent.

Presently, for your WordPress-built site, you have only a welcome page created but nothing else so far. Also, we haven't posted anything online. (We'll be doing that near the end of this chapter.) You're going to want to make a post introducing yourself and your future blog. This inaugural post can be as detailed and as informative as you like; but the more people who know about you and what your blog is about, the more likely you will pick up subscribers.

Completing Your Pages

Before we approach proper blogging—creating posts reflecting your thoughts, opinions, and deep analysis of a topic of interest or expertise—we want to finish up the Pages of our WordPress-powered site. As Pages are static, these are places where we offer up static information like contact information, upcoming appearances, published works, and the like. WordPress has already set up a few Pages for you. Let's go on and work with these templates, and finish up our website.

STEP 1 From your Dashboard, single-click the "Site" option. From the expanded menu, single-click the "Pages" option.

Your Dashboard, as seen in Figure 1-3, displays all your current Pages. From here, you can edit the various pages that will make up your website.

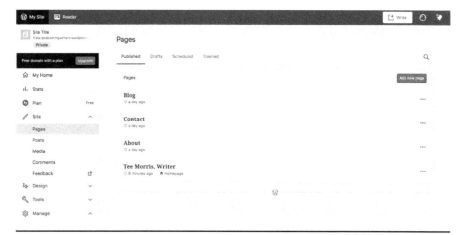

Figure 1-3: Pages are those sections of your website and blog that are not updated as often as the main blog section. Pages can include contact information, upcoming appearances for the year, and the like.

STEP 2   Single-click the "Contact" page.

STEP 3   Select the "Contact" title and add your name.

STEP 4   Single-click inside the "Don't hesitate…" text block and edit this welcome message to read the way you want it to read.

STEP 5   Single-click the "Get in Touch" title and then single-click More Options. Select "Remove Block" from the drop menu.

STEP 6   Single-click inside the mock address, and repeat Step 5.

STEP 7   Repeat Step 5 for the Form and the "Send Us a Message" header.

Right now, we are keeping it simple for our Pages. Forms are a way of having visitors to your site answer specific questions or requests. You can learn more about forms from WordPress, but let's stick to the basics right now. The grey box left behind is part of the Page's template. Don't worry about seeing it. On going live, it will not be visible.

STEP 8   Single-click to the right of the email. Then edit the email to be your own.

The content block you are working with here is the Email Block. Any email entered in here will automatically be formatted. No HTML editing necessary.

STEP 9   Single-click to the right of the phone number. Repeat Step 5 for the Phone Block.

STEP 10   At the bottom of the Contact page is a row of social media icons. Single-click the "Add Block" tool (the plus sign) and, as pictured in Figure 1-4, review the various social media platforms recognized by this template.

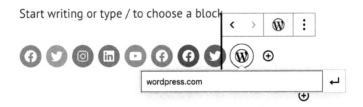

Figure 1-4: The Social Links tool covers a variety of platforms. Select from the menu any platform you wish to add.

STEP 11 Click on the WordPress icon (the "W") and then single-click More Options. Select "Remove Block" from the drop menu.

STEP 12 Click on the Twitter icon (the bird) to view the "Edit Link" option underneath it.

This is where you would enter your own social media links. By default, the Social Link blocks are set to the home site of the platform. After you establish your links, come back to this page and edit as needed.

STEP 13 Single-click the "Update" button and, when done, single-click the "Preview" button to the left of it. Click the "Close" button to return to editing.

Figure 1-5: The Preview mode offers you a sneak peek at what your page will look like before you go live with it.

STEP 14 Single-click the "View Pages" option, located at the top-left corner.

Okay, so that was a lot of steps to go through to get such a sparse-looking webpage, but this webpage not only has a lot of functionality within it, this design is a basic one. You can always build on it in the future. Right now, we are learning to crawl before we walk. So far, the Welcome and the Contact Pages are ready to go. Now, let's create a short biography page that introduces yourself to the world.

STEP 1 From the Pages menu, single-click the "About" page.

The About Page is a "This is who I am…" page. No need to be shy. Let people know at a glance who you are, what you write, and where you are from.

 While social media is all about sharing, keep in mind you do not have to share everything. It's important to draw boundaries and keep some details close to the vest so you don't give away too much about yourself or where you live. Privacy is a beautiful thing to protect.

STEP 2   Single-click the "About" title. Add your name to it.

STEP 3   Single-click the "Introduce yourself…" header, and edit it to a simple subtitle that describes you.

STEP 4   Single-click inside the text block. Add in a simple bio, no more than 100-200 words, about yourself. (You can always expand on it later.)

Lessons Learned as a Dummies Author

Figure 1-6: By clicking on blocks of content, as seen in this blogpost, a menu of Block Options appears. These various options help you designate what kind of content block you are working with.

STEP 5   Single-click the sample photo and from the menu provided, select the "Replace" option. From the drop menu, select the "Upload" option.

STEP 6   Find on your computer a good headshot and drop it into place. A good headshot image for a template like this one should be no bigger than 1000 x 1000 pixels in size with a resolution of 72 pixels per inch.

STEP 7   Single-click the "Update" button and, when done, single-click the "Preview" button to the left of it. Click the "Close" button to return to editing.

As seen in Figure 1-7, the bio page should be short and sweet. You can, if you want, expand on this with other aspects of your life; but on starting out, focus on who you are and what you write. Editing after a page goes live is the easy part.

About Tee

Writer. Podcaster. Streamer.

Tee Morris has been writing science fiction, fantasy, horror, and non-fiction for over a decade. His debut novel, *MOREVI: The Chronicles of Rafe & Askana*, became the first novel to be podcast in its entirety, ushering in a new age for authors — podcasting. He went on with Evo Terra to write *Podcasting for Dummies* (as well as the 2nd Edition alongside Chuck Tomasi). In 2011, Tee returned to fiction with the Ministry of Peculiar Occurrences series, penned with his wife, Pip Ballantine. The series and its short fiction podcast, *Tales from the Archives*, has won several awards including the RT Reviews' Choice Awards for Best Steampunk of 2014; and inspired the Y.A. spin-off series, *Verity Fitzroy and the Ministry Seven*. And somewhere in the middle of all that, Tee reunited with Chuck Tomasi for the third edition of *Podcasting for Dummies* in 2017 and wrote *Twitch for Dummies* on his own in 2019.

Figure 1-7: When putting together an About page, your first draft should be something simple. You can always expand on it if you feel the need to share more.

STEP 8   Single-click the "View Pages" option, located at the top-left corner.

All that remains now on your website is the Blog Page. The Blog, on looking at it in preview mode, is a page that offers snippets of blogposts. Clicking on the title, you are rerouted to that individual blog post. As the blog moderator, you will be able to compose and edit blogposts.

Producing Content

Understanding the WordPress interface and its content blocks is easy. The hard part is sticking with an editorial calendar. A blog without regular, consistent content does not represent a writer in the best light. It gets even harder to produce content if you are working on a deadline. After all, instead of blogging about writing, shouldn't you be writing? This is the common argument writers of all genres, of all backgrounds, have against blogging and its value. Truth is that, yes, your priority should be your commissions—those projects that come with editors, publishers, deadlines, and paychecks; and low on the priority list, along with other items pushed to the edge of your desk, sits your blog on the Internet, silently mocking you.

Blogging shouldn't be a chore or hindrance from your writing career. It is your best introduction to potential readers and your direct connection to your audience. With the right strategy, keeping your content lively, relevant, and consistent on your blog can easily fall into your writing routine. And if your projects take priority, you can let people know a break is imminent; or catch people up after an unexpected break.

Your first blog posts should introduce readers to you and also begin establishing yourself as someone with knowledge worth reading and sharing. The actual promotion of your new blog, though, should not come until you have content within reach, polished, edited, and ready to schedule.

Here are a few ideas on blog topics:

- When I'm Not Writing (travel, interests, hobbies, or how you unplug)
- Authors That Inspire Me
- What Inspires My Writing
- Favorite Books (different genres, all time, repeat reads)
- Creating Characters You Love or Hate
- Software/Hardware for Writers (can also include productivity tips, research tools, etc.)

The above topics produce what is known as evergreen content. These are blog posts that can easily be rotated in and out of an editorial calendar in case of something topical or breaking news (a new book contract, a news headline from the publishing industry) comes to your attention. Evergreen content can also be repurposed which means a blog post can be tweaked, rewritten, and edited for guest postings on other blogs. The more posts you have like this on hand, the more content you have in case you find yourself running tight on time and short on blog topics. Before launching your blog, schedule five evergreen posts for yourself.

In your WordPress "beginner blog" are three identical posts. If you were to go live with your blog, these three posts will go live under your name. Not the best way to make a good first impression. So let's edit one of these posts, and then remove the other two.

STEP 1   From your Dashboard, single-click the "Site" option. From the expanded menu, single-click the "Posts" option.

STEP 2   Click within any of the paragraphs in this mock blog post. Click on a different paragraph. Then click on a third. Notice the "Text Block" tools you have access to.

Text Blocks offer a variety of formatting options. You can bold text, italicize text, create hyperlinks, change alignment, and other changes to your text. Within a text block, you can fine tune your text to read exactly the way you want it to read.

STEP 3   Click anywhere into the top text block that begins with "This is an example post…" and from "More Options" tool, select the "Remove Block" option.

STEP 4   Click anywhere in the text block that begins with "You're going to publish a post…" and go to "Command + A" (Mac) or "Control + A" (PC) on your keyboard to select all the text in the block. Replace the selected text with the following:

This is my first blog entry. I am now officially getting my hands dirty in social media, learning how initiatives like blogging works but I will be getting into Facebook, Twitter, and other networks as well. It's going to be a long day, but I can see now just how easy it is to write for a blog. How cool is that?

STEP 5   Repeat Step 3 for all the text blocks underneath the one you just edited in Step 4.

STEP 6   Click inside the "Introduce Yourself" text block and edit it to read "Welcome to my new blog!" as your title for this blogpost.

STEP 7   Single-click the "Update" button, and take a look at your first blogpost, as seen in Figure 1-8.

Figure 1-8: A simple blogpost, created from the three originally created by WordPress.

STEP 8   Single-click the "View Pages" option, located at the top-left corner.

STEP 9   Look to the far-right of the three blogposts and you will see an "Options" menu (three dots) there. Single-click the Options menu on one of the "Introduce Yourself" example posts. Select "Trash" from the Options menu.

STEP 10 Repeat Step 9 for the last remaining starter post, and close the notifications that appear, if visible.

This is working with pre-existing blogposts. You can get an idea of how editing works when you have a post already put together, but let's go a little deeper and talk about workflow. How do we do this from scratch? This particular exercise will require a blogpost written in your word processor of choice.

STEP 1   Launch your word processor and write up a blogpost. Feel free to add in active hyperlinks. The word count for your posts should be between 500-1000 words long.

There is no real set-in-stone length for blogposts. Some people blog between 100-300 words and others blog well beyond 2000 words. It all depends on the topic you are blogging about. Find a good length for you and your blogs, and work to stay within those parameters.

STEP 2 After writing up your new blogpost, go back and edit. Look for typos, grammatical errors, and clarity. When you are finished editing, save your work.

While you could compose your blogpost in WordPress, writing and editing a post is actually easier on the eyes and the brain than trying to work in the blog GUI. Additionally, WordPress' GUI is easy enough in making a blogpost happen, it tends to feel a bit clumsy when compared to a word processor. Take advantage of your ease and comfort with your favorite writing program when composing new blogposts.

 Some writers take their blogposts and publish them as a collection of thoughts, writing advice, and humorous rants on a variety of topics, many of them based in writing and the writer's life. If you have blogposts saved in other text formats, they can be easier to edit, layout, and publish, than exporting published blogposts into an editable format.

STEP 3 Return to WordPress on your browser. Single-click the "Add New Post" button.

STEP 4 Where you see the "Add Title" content block, type in the title of your blog.

STEP 5 Go back to your word processor and select the entire blogpost. Click on "Start writing or type…" and then use "Command + C" (Mac) or "Control + C" (PC)_to copy it.

STEP 6 Return to WordPress and single-click "V" (Mac) or "Control + V" (PC)_to paste your blogpost.

STEP 7 Scroll back to the top of your blogpost and begin a final review process.

STEP 8 Look for a break between paragraphs where a picture would look good. Click the "Add content block" tool and single-click it.

STEP 9 Select "Image" as the style of content block you want to add. From the new content block, single-click the "Upload" button.

STEP 10 Search for an appropriate image on your computer from the window that appears, and click "Open" to upload it.

Any images uploaded on to WordPress is kept in an image gallery where you can use media in your blogposts repeatedly.

STEP 11   Click "Save Draft" to save your blogpost.

You now have your first original blogpost ready for publication. It's only a draft right now, and we're not going to make it live right away. We are going to take advantage of the scheduling tool so we can have content go live when we want it rather than straight away. This way, you can produce three blogposts but space them out over time.

STEP 1   In the blogpost you just created, single-click the "Settings" tool (the gear wheel) and single-click the "Document" tab.
Settings is a simple tool that accesses the preferences of the content block you are working with or the blogpost itself.

STEP 2   Look for where you see the "Publish" option. To the right of it, you see "Immediately" as the publishing option. Single-click "Immediately" to access scheduling options.

STEP 3   Select date and set a time for posting in the following week, as seen in Figure 1-9.

Figure 1-9: When your blogpost is ready to post, take a look at the Schedule option. Pick a good day to have your thoughts go live, and then single-click the "Schedule . . ." button.

STEP 4   After reviewing, click the "Schedule" button at the top.

STEP 5   Single-click the "View Pages" option, located at the top-left corner. You can still access and edit the scheduled post by going to "Scheduled" and accessing it there.

STEP 6   Single-click "My Home" in the left sidebar and single-click the "Launch site" button.

Welcome to your first blog. You've got Pages live with your bio, ways to contact you, and more. You also have a live blogpost for people to see, and another waiting in the wings for publication. Where you go from here is entirely up to you.

Posting Frequency

So now that you have a blog, your next step is to grab hold of that audience out there just waiting to find you. The big question: how often should you post?

Bloggers often think of themselves as baseball players coming out of the batter's circle swinging two bats—only in the blogger's case it's two blog posts instead of two bats. If you stocked up on evergreen posts (let's say five, standing by ready to go) and then you created two more timely posts, you may think two posts a week would work. That sounds easy but it is actually an ambitious plan when you break it down. First, this plan would burn through the evergreen content you created within the course of just one month. If you blink, you'll suddenly find yourself short on content.

When first launching a blog, aim for weekly or bi-weekly posts. Pick a day and make that the day you post on your blog. It can be difficult to maintain that schedule, and it could be a bit frustrating trying to build an audience. The advantage is getting a complete idea of what it is like to produce content for a blog on a regular basis. This kind of schedule also allows you latitude to reschedule evergreen topics in light of topics you want to post in the moment.

When you find a rhythm to posting content, you can always add to your content and offer up spontaneous postings when you feel inspired, or themes for different days of the week. "Monday Motivation" features your favorite motivational quotes from your favorite authors while "Tuesday Teasers" are selections from your upcoming book release or perhaps a work-in-progress closing in on completion. Themed posts — whether text, an image, or both — are great for simple, quick content that are easily syndicated on other blogs and publicized on various social networks.

 With a graphic as a post, it can be easily featured on visual platforms like Instagram and Pinterest. Make sure the image you post is:

- Formatted not as a portrait or landscape but in a perfect square. Instagram, in particular, features all their pictures in equal ratios.
- Original photography or artwork created by you, or...
- Royalty-free images that you have purchased. Use of copyrighted material, including imagery, without proper permissions can land you in trouble if you're using it to promote your work. Branded with your website so when the image is shared, others will know where it originates.

These images can be created in a variety of mobile and desktop applications like ImageQuote. You will find out more about ImageQuote in Chapter 5.

Additional Blogging Strategies

After blogging twice a week for some time, you will establish yourself as a source of regular, reliable content. Why not, then, reach out to other writers and offer them a place to share their thoughts? Invite other authors to write on topics you think your audience would enjoy, or let them take your blog for a day and speak their mind on topics they come up with but that you approve. Once a topic is agreed upon, schedule your guest or guests accordingly. Keep your guest posts within reasonable word count parameters—500 to 1,000 words—and give them a day you don't normally post. Depending on how many people you want to offer a moment on your blog, you may have guest blog posts alternate with blogs of your own content. If you find yourself with many volunteers, step up the frequency and aim for a weekly feature of a new voice from your corner of the Internet.

Why would you want to invite other authors to blog? Guest blogging benefits both you and your guests on several levels. For you, your blog gets fresh, new content, a completely different voice, and a touch of variety. You also get the opportunity to introduce your blog to a new audience—your guest's. Your guests, on the other hand, are given the chance to introduce themselves and their work to your audience, so it's a win-win for both parties. The guest feature also allows guests to play the role of expert on whatever particular topic you have asked them to blog about. Finally, appearing on a blog other than their own, guests increase their reach, and in turn increase their search results, proving they are not exclusive to their own blog.

Another way of introducing new content to your blog is to host a *blog tour*. Unlike a bookstore or convention tour, a blog tour takes place in the comfort of your own home. Your travel itinerary consists of various stops across the blogosphere. On a blog tour, you guest post on other blogs, talking about your book and its relevant topics, all the while inviting the blog hosts to appear on your blog. This pay-it-forward approach to blogging and publicity is a great way to get your words in front of potential readers and to spread the word about your works.

You can get a blog tour rolling in two ways: pay for someone to organize it or do the work of organizing it yourself.

 There are two kinds of blog tours. One kind of tour is just you, hopping from blog to blog, as if you were traveling from bookstore to bookstore on a standard promotional tour. The other approach is to schedule a book tour between several different authors and build a round-robin of visits so that everyone in the tour visits everyone else's site. For a first-time tour, make a round-robin with no more than eight authors.

Book bloggers who arrange blog tours for authors can earn a good amount of income. Price tags for these services vary, but one thing is certain: hiring a tour manager costs you the lowest in stress. Also, tour hosts usually know more bloggers and writers to approach than you do, making your investment a wise one.

You can put out the call to authors in your network, of course. Using Google Docs or Microsoft Excel is the best way to keep track of participants and to schedule dates for your participants. Just remember: Whether hosting or participating, you are investing time and resources in keeping others and yourself on track. You do not want to miss an appearance or fail to produce a piece. People are relying on you for content, just as you are relying on others.

When your next stop on a blog tour comes up, your host may have interview questions already lined up for you; but sometimes you may have to come up with your own topic for a blog stop. Thinking up ideas for these can occasionally be hard, especially if you are on a long blog tour and feel as if you cannot come up with another idea. Here are some to get you started:

- Who would you cast in the movie based on your book, and why?
- What is your inspiration for this book?
- What is it about the setting for this book that you find compelling?
- Go deep into the motivations of your favorite character.
- Plotter or pantser? How do you map out a book?
- What is your typical day as a writer?
- Who are your literary influences, and why?
- Lessons learned from working on a title.
- What I love about my cover.

These are reliable topics that hosts love to feature on blog tours. Pitch two or three of them to your upcoming stop, and see what they want. If they say "It's up to you…" pick a favorite and run with it. At the end of the tour, you will have a wider reach for your name and your work.

You will also have, at the end of the tour, new evergreen content ready for repurposing and posting on your own blog. Give your new content considerable time (at the very least, six months) from the end of the tour before you start posting this content.

Syndicating Content

In the same way that podcasting is defined in a variety of ways (Chapter 7), bloggers tend to define syndication in different ways. For this book, we define syndication as taking the opening paragraph of another's blog post and featuring it on your own blog. You then add a link that reads "To read the entire blog post, follow this link…" from your blog to the original blog post's origin. Syndicating a blog post provides your own blog content while directing traffic to another blog.

The optimal way to syndicate a blog post is to feature a post up to the point where the post's home blog breaks between two paragraphs using the "Read More…" attribute. The "Read More…" attribute creates a unique URL that picks up where the previous paragraph leaves off. Using this link, you can have people start a blog post at one location, and end at another.

While syndicating blogs is a terrific way to encourage community between blogs in the process of sharing, syndication should happen only on occasion. Blog syndication should not be your only source of secondary content, and it should never be your sole source of content. As stated earlier, people are coming to your blog to hear your voice. If your idea of blogging is nothing more than collecting the thoughts of others, readers may find themselves asking why they are coming to your website for any reason beyond picking up blogging resources that produce original content.

WordPress has a lot to offer. With just a little investment of time to learn how it works, you can create for yourself a strong basis for all of your social media. There are other features worth exploring with your blogposts like tags, meta descriptions, featured images, and other options that help with your blog's visibility. After getting a grasp on the basics of WordPress, go exploring with its other functions. Play with themes, establish categories, and —most importantly — produce content consistent with you and your blog. It will be here we begin to build on your brand.

What will your blog say about you?

II: TUMBLR

DRIVE-BY BLOGGING

The founder and CEO of Tumblr, David Karp, set out to make something less verbose and easier to handle than WordPress. Even though he said that Tumblr was made for "those who don't like writing," that doesn't mean writers can't make the most out of this platform. In fact, it could be the most useful platform for those with limited time, who still want to reach an engaged and youthful audience.

Tumblr might have started out as a way to do short-form blogging, but it has become huge itself—and quite popular, with over 171 billion posts.

The ease of use and the quickness with which users can share information make it attractive to a wide audience.

On Tumblr, users share all sorts of things they find interesting (such as images, audio, quotes, and short passages from books). They comment on posts, share, reblog, and build a community around their information.

When you first look at the stream of constant Tumblr information, it can be a little daunting. It flows through your feed like Twitter, but with more images, moving images, and videos. Your job is to put your information into the stream, but it has to be engaging and visually exciting to attract attention.

Some authors blog only with Tumblr instead of WordPress, while some use both. It's up to each individual to decide how much time they have available to them.

If you are short on time or find long-form blogging hard to get into, then Tumblr could be a good platform for you.

What is the Difference Between WordPress and Tumblr?

If WordPress is writing a letter to the world, then Tumblr is the postcard version: Tumblr blogs have a pretty picture and contain generally shorter posts about how your day has gone. Tumblr is also easier and quicker to read, and the post's recipient often shows it to other people. If you are lucky, the recipient will pin it onto his refrigerator…which, in this case, is another Tumblr account.

Deeper down there are other differences, too.

While WordPress can either host your content or allow you to host it on your own site, Tumblr is more of a mash-up of a social network—think of it as WordPress and Twitter joining forces. The advantage Tumblr has over Twitter is that with Tumblr you have more than 280 characters to work with. So Tumblr allows you to show more of your personality than Twitter does. Make good use of this feature, because personality means a lot to those on Tumblr, but remember to keep it brief. Tumblr readers like to scan their feeds.

The other difference is that Tumblr is a stand-alone company, whereas WordPress is open source. This means that a community of developers are free to work on WordPress, contribute to changes, and offer a variety of themes and plug-in's to broaden its capabilities. Tumblr allows the user some freedom, like personalizing their page, but it is not nearly as expansive as WordPress. This creates some restrictions in how you can organize and present content.

Tumblr offers a social aspect that WordPress does not. You can "like" and reblog posts, follow people who interest you, and make comments on posts, which is important in social media. Interaction on any network means people are taking notice of you, and better still, sharing your words with their audience. Interaction is what makes social media so much fun, as well as so different from the early days of the Internet. Sharing is not just caring, but also brings more eyeballs to what you are saying and, in turn, to your books.

Why Tumblr?

If you are a writer with limited time, Tumblr is a quick and easy way to share a variety of content. If you have a beautiful image to share or a snippet of audio from your work, then this is the place to be. There are plenty of eager eyeballs just waiting for it. The social aspect of Tumblr means you can connect with other readers and writers who share your interests. Building networks is one of the strengths of this platform; it's not just about posting your work.

If you want to use Tumblr as your main Web presence for blogging, you can also add pages. You might consider adding pages that detail your appearances or your biography, for instance.

In short, Tumblr gives you more space to work with than Twitter, and it is quicker and easier to fit into your day than WordPress. If you are not comfortable operating all the bells and whistles you get with WordPress, yet you want to have some measure of customization, then Tumblr could be a good option for you.

A great thing about social media is that you can enjoy the best of both worlds. There are WordPress plug-in's that will simultaneously create a post on Tumblr. The post is a selection of the opening paragraph, followed by the link that takes readers to the blog. It is not necessarily the same as posting original content on Tumblr, but it can assure you that content is reaching your Tumblr account.

So why not have your cake and eat it, too?

Wider Audience

Writers want to go where the readers are; and if you are looking for a young, engaged demographic, Tumblr is the place. According to Tumblr, 43% of their users are eighteen and twenty-four years old. So if your genre appeals to that demographic, it's time to jump into the Tumblr stream. Even if your readers are older, Tumbler has plenty of those users, too: 30% are over forty-five, while Millennials make up a third of its users. Tumblr is also different from most other social media sites in that it's pretty evenly divided between genders. (https://financesonline.com/number-of-tumblr-blogs/)

Ease of Use

The Tumblr action bar makes it simple to use. Text, Photo, Quote, Link, Chat, Audio, and Video are options laid at your fingertips. You can upload your content directly from your website or another person's website, or you can just drag the image to upload it. Tumblr works hard to keep it easy.

Don't forget your Tumblr page and profile says a lot about you, so get in there immediately and customize it. Make this corner of the Internet your own. You can tweak the colors of your page or go for a theme that you can adjust to your style. The more original and unique your Tumblr presence, the more people will want to follow your blog. Many of Tumblr's customizations are offered as free choices, but there are some that you can pay for as well.

With Tumblr, you can also create a group blog where more than one person can post. You can assign members and then promote a few of its contributors (or all of them) to administrator (admin) roles, granting them the ability to invite new users, remove current ones, delete posts, and reply to messages. Regular members can add their own posts, as well as edit or delete them. Group Tumblrs are good if you are co-writing a book with another author, or if you are writing an anthology. However, only secondary blogs (described below) can be group blogs.

Setting up a Tumblr Account

Tumblr is one of the easiest social media platforms to work with. To set up an account, follow these instructions.

Figure 2-1: Your entry to the world of Tumblr

STEP 1   Go to www.tumblr.com, enter a valid e-mail address, make yourself a username (keep it simple; using your author name is a good idea), and create a password.

STEP 2   Once you've told them how old you are, accepted their terms of service, and proved you are not a robot, Tumblr creates an account for you.

STEP 3   Tumblr will then ask you what you are interested in and prompt you to start following five blogs. You can follow some of the suggested blogs or search for others to follow using terms such as "writing," "authors" or your genre. Don't worry, the more you follow, the more you'll feel a part of the community, so feel free to select more than five.

STEP 4   You will have to confirm your e-mail address in order to customize.

STEP 5   Click on the head icon in the top-left corner and then click on "Edit Appearance."

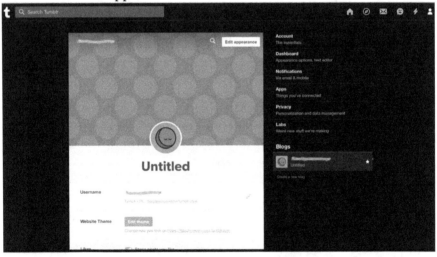

Figure 2-2: Let's make your Tumblr look more like you want it. Use an avatar of yourself, and then tweak the color scheme. Title and description are optional but useful.

STEP 6   Next you can download the Tumblr app for IOS, Android, or Windows Phone. You don't have to do it now, but it is a great app to have at your fingertips.

And voila, there you are in your Dashboard. Don't panic: This is not how the viewing public will see your Tumblr, but it is where you will be spending some time managing and sprucing up your account.

Though this initial setup generates your primary blog, you can in fact have multiple blogs in the form of secondary accounts, and/or add pages to any of these blogs. You might want to consider using your primary as your writer account, with different pages for your series. Or you might want to have secondary blogs for your series, especially if you are co-writing them. Again, you may be splitting your brand too much, so decide how fractured you want your Tumblr content to be.

Getting to Know Tumblr

Let's go ahead and get familiar with the Tumblr controls. There are several key areas.

Figure 2-3: Tumblr's primary toolbar

The top bar

Home. This will take you back to the main dashboard and your stream.

Explore. This will bring you to the browse section of Tumblr. Here you can see trending topics, categories, and staff picks. A great place to find blogs to follow.

Inbox. This is where you will get messages from your Tumblr followers, questions, submissions, and fan mail. Keep an eye on this icon to alert you to these valuable interactions.

Messages. Here you will find your direct messages, that are not publicly viewable.

Lightning Bolt. This will take you to your activity page, where you can see how engaged people are with what you are posting, your biggest fans (people who engage or repost your posts the most), and the latest comments on your posts. It's fun to watch the graphs here.

Head Icon. This is the home base for all of your content. This shows you how many posts you have made, how many followers you have, what activity has occurred since you last checked (along with a neat chart of how your posts are doing), how many items you have lined up in your queue, and, most importantly, it offers the ability to customize your page. Clicking on the head icon and then Edit Appearance will allow you to change your page to your liking. Much like WordPress, Tumblr has themes, frameworks so you can easily set up the look of your blog. Some are free, some available to purchase, but there are so many themes that finding something for yourself and your genre is a definite possibility. After you click on Edit Theme, you will see what your Tumblr looks like to the public. On the left, you will see your options. These will vary according to the theme you have selected. You can use this to add static pages to your Tumblr. You might, for example, want to have a separate page for an About page or perhaps a list of events you are attending.

The Pen. Click this for all the options you need to post content. The next bar is our favorite.

The Content bar

Figure 2-4: Tumblr's content bar is how you format text and incorporate media with your posts.

Adding your own content to your Tumblr stream is always the preferable option, so let's take a quick look at the ways you can do it:

Text. Create a title and write your content in the field at the bottom. You can also format your text in a variety of ways, including making those all-important links back to your site or where to buy your book.

Photos. Here you can upload photos, or take one directly with the camera in your computer. Remember: Images are your best friend in Tumblr.

Quote. Use this to add little teasers from your work-in-progress or novel that's about to come out. Make sure they are punchy quotes that express the content of your book or main character.

URL. This is where you link to your WordPress site or to reviews of your books. Unfortunately you can't use an image with this option, so you might want to use it sparingly.

Chat. Used to solicit commentary and that important engagement. Could be used to chat with your readers and ask them their opinions, favorite characters, etc.

Audio. This is where you would post podcasts, or recordings of your story. Samples of your audiobook would be an excellent choice to upload—just remember to keep them up to 10MB, and that they must be in MP3 format. You can search for a track to post, upload directly, or share from a URL. Do be sure to fill in all the fields and to have a good cover image for maximum impact.

Video. If you have a book trailer, this is where you can upload it directly (if it's 100MB or less in size and five minutes long), or you can either put in the code (say from YouTube) or the URL where the video can be found. Same rules on filling all the fields apply.

 No matter what you upload, do not forget to supply the relevant hashtags to draw attention to your post.

Each of these offers different advanced options, but the most useful ones are Schedule and Add to Queue. These are some of Tumblr's best features for authors since they allow you to target a post to go live at an important moment—say on a book launch date—or pop a post in a feed to be delivered on a regular schedule. Remember your readers like consistency with their content!

Reblogging

Sometimes you just don't have enough original content to feed the hunger of Tumblr, or you want to spread out what you do have. In our Ministry of Peculiar Occurrences Tumblr, we do three reblogs to one original post. By using this ratio you will avoid constantly shouting *"Buy my book!!!"* into the void.

Reblogging also offers the advantage of building a following. Everyone whose post you reblog sees that you've reblogged their post, after all. So let's have a go at reblogging some content.

The blogs you are following are now showing up in your dashboard in a stream, with the newest at the top. Find something useful and relevant to your audience.

At the top of the post are a few icons. The paper plane lets you send the post to someone. The chat circle lets you add a note to the post. On the very right is the Heart icon, which is how you favorite the post. It's a nice way to show a sense of community and will help your account get noticed, but reposting is even better.

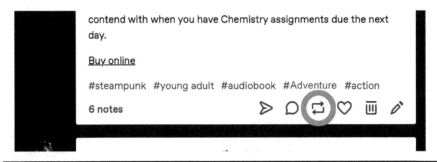

contend with when you have Chemistry assignments due the next day.

Buy online

#steampunk #young adult #audiobook #Adventure #action

6 notes

Figure 2-5: The *Reblogging* icon for is two circling arrows. Reblogging is a fantastic way to build a community of goodwill and cross-promotion in your Tumblr network.

This is the icon that will post the item into your Tumblr feed. Clicking on it will bring the post you want to reblog up in full. Here you can add your own tags, put the post into your queue, schedule it, or post it right away. We urge you to add your own commentary to the item before you post, just to let people know that you are not some robot mindlessly reposting items. For our steampunk series we usually try to say something that will link the item back to the series. If we see a vehicle the Ministry might use, we point that out. That way, you are bringing it back to your brand without hijacking the content. Always remember to leave whatever attribution there is on the post intact.

When you set up your Tumblr account, you establish a profile as well as your primary blog. The primary blog can be hosted only by the profile holder. Secondary blogs, as explained above, allow for multiple admins. Tumblr allows you to have as many secondary blogs as you desire; but your primary blog only allows for one administrator.

Another little time-saver is the Tumblr extension, available for both Chrome and Firefox browsers. Whenever you see something interesting on a website, you simply click the extension icon. It will open post form in a new window. This nifty little device even grabs video and images. It also links back to the source, but lets you add your own commentary. (Remember, Tumblr wants to make blogging as easy as possible.)

The Tumblr extension is a great time-saving device that allows you to share interesting items you find quickly and easily. And that's wonderful, because who doesn't love getting things done with less effort?

 Readers cannot comment on your Tumblr blog, but if you install the third-party expansion Disqus (https://disqus.com), then you can have that functionality on your blog. First, create a Disqus account, then go to your Tumblr click "Edit Appearance.", and then 'Edit Theme". Then on the left under "Theme Options," enter the Disqus Shortname and click "Save." Now your readers will have the option to comment, just like they do on WordPress.

Mobile Possibilities

Tumblr's app is available for all your smartphones—after all, Tumblr is about sharing and in some instances, that means on the go. Readers love to see a slice of your life, especially if you are rubbing shoulders with other authors. The app offers all the features of the website optimized for your iPhone, Android, or tablets. Like all other social media platforms, it is up to you to decide how much you want to share; rest assured, the Tumblr app is just as easy to use as its website sibling. If you want to take advantage of "Tumbling" while out in the wild, dive into the Tumblr app and keep your readers in the know.

 WordPress is not the only platform that plays well with Tumblr. Many authors connect their Tumblr account to their Instagram account. You can easily sync your Tumblr from the Instagram app, just as you can for Twitter and Facebook. Find out more about Instagram and how you can cross-post on the platform with Tumblr in Chapter 5.

What should you post to share with your readers?

- *Travel.* If you're going somewhere interesting—even if it's just your morning walk—snap a picture and upload it.
- *Food.* Pictures of tasty things make for great Tumblr posts.
- *Events.* Let people know you're accessible.
- *Artwork.* What inspires you? A steampunk fashion shoot? An iconic comic book panel? A classic piece from J.M.W. Turner or Georges Seurat? Post it!
- *Animated GIFs.* We dare you to search Tumblr for animated GIFs of Tom Hiddleston. Go on. (Just make sure you have a few hours.) For fun, you can also look for author related GIFs, like famous authors writing, and pages turning.
- *Pets.* The Internet wasn't invented for animals, but sometimes it sure feels that way. Posting pics of your pooch shows your softer side, plus it offers a bit of your personal life without using pictures of your children.

You might think these things don't apply to you, especially if you are just embarking on your writing career. But you'd be surprised how interested readers are in seeing inside a writer's life—even if you're a "new" writer. No matter how long you've been at it, it is good to establish yourself as a real person, not just a writing machine.

Expressing Yourself: Producing Content

Photo and video content are the most reblogged and shared posts on Tumblr. They catch the eye and are more likely to stop readers who are scanning through posts. If you have posted something visual, you immediately have an advantage over the posts that are text only. Just be sure to link back to your website or other authors links. Otherwise you are wasting an opportunity. The other content that Tumblr users love, as listed above, are Animated Graphic Interchange Format images, or Animated GIFs. Love them or loathe them, refer to them using a hard or soft g pronunciation, on this platform they rule, particularly if they feature pop culture. If you feel like spicing up your blog with GIFs, then you may want to check out the website, Giphy (http://giphy.com). There are plenty of wonderful, funny GIFs related to writing, writers, and beloved books; and Tumblr has a very active and passionate reading community.

But how do writers use Tumblr? Neil Gaiman uses his Tumblr account (https://neil-gaiman.tumblr.com) purely as a way to interact with fans. He reposts questions sent to him, and then adds answers at the bottom. If you have enough of a fan base on the site, then this is a great way of reaching out to them. Kiera Cass (http://partylikeawordstar.tumblr.com) author of the Selection Series, posts all about boy bands, fun happenings with her series (lots of images for example), and best of all, answers questions from her fans. So if you hear other writers say, *"Writers aren't on Tumblr..."* that could not be farther from the truth. Tumblr is a great place for writers to express themselves, promote themselves, and have a bit of fun.

Don't forget to use hashtags with your original content, as this is an easy way others are going to find your content. Our Ministry podcasts we post to Tumblr for an example we would tag #steampunk #podcast #adventure #mystery and add in a tag about any location in the podcast like #Berlin or #Ireland. Hashtags are your friend on Tumblr, like many other social media platforms. Be sure to include many tags, but remember only the first twenty will actually work—that's a lot of space to operate in. Popular tags include topics on fashion, vintage, film, makeup, and animals.

When producing content, you want to make use of Tumblr's best features: Queue and Schedule. Schedule lets you pick the time and day you want your post to go out. Queue grants you the ability to add a post to a collection of posts that will go out at set times. For example, you can adjust your settings to drop a fresh post from your queue once, twice, or as many times a day as you want. Tumblr also lets you set the time parameters of when you want the posts to happen. You can choose how often each of these posts from the queue fires off. Twice a day is a popular choice, but you can post into your queue up to fifty times a day if you want to—or are able to. We recommend two to five posts per day. Don't flood your feed, but don't leave it idle either.

Reblogging and Original Content: Which is Best?

Though it's generally simpler than blogging, using Tumblr still requires a time commitment. There are writers who cue up original content or sync up their blogs with Tumblr in order to share their most recent posts in a feed, while other authors reblog the content of others and are happy with producing a highlight reel of all the "cool stuff" they've found on their own.

Reblogging others' content is a great way to build a community and display interesting items in your own feed. However, you also need to add your own commentary, so readers see you interacting with the post rather than mindlessly reblogging. If the comment ties the content into your own work as well, bonus points.

We want to stress that original content is not merely a link to "buy my book" (though it can contain a link to buy).

 There's an art to subtly advertising your book. You want to make it easy to find, but you don't want to hit people over the head with it either. Usually when we share images, we also include a short paragraph from the work, and below that a link to where people can buy.

Original content can be pictures of your day, observations of things around you, conventions or conferences, and people you meet. It can also be snippets from your published book or one you are working on. Tumblr readers want to learn something interesting and insightful about you and your writing.

What to Expect from the Tumblr Community

To become part of the community, you need to make connections and participate. Standing on the sidelines simply doesn't make you friends. Don't be afraid to make the first move. When you first create your account, you need to find connections and start working on them immediately. Tumblr will suggest accounts for you to follow in the sidebar, basing its suggestions on the keywords you use to tag your content with and the accounts you are currently following. Take a closer look at what is suggested and start building your network right away.

Show your personality by following people outside of the writing community. In this way, you can display what a well-rounded person you are. Readers are interested in people who write and what they do beyond typing. Insights make you interesting.

You can also look for blogs by doing a keyword search: travel, history, food. Tumblr features accounts on anything and everything. Tumblr lets you follow two hundred accounts a day, or five thousand different Tumblrs total for each Tumblr you manage. Don't be shy about following all you can. The more you follow, the more people will follow you in turn.

Don't forget to like (or heart) and reblog from your new connections—that way you are spreading the love and encouraging them to like and reblog your posts as well. When you start to get comments on your posts, be sure to respond to them.

Remember: Interaction is the key. You're cultivating a community.

Sharing with the Class: Syndicating Media

Sharing your information across various platforms makes for easy content. Since Tumblr has a different audience and community from other platforms, don't be afraid to repost content you are featuring on other locations such as your blog, Instagram, or Facebook.

As you will find throughout this book and online, media is the content that earns you the most traffic. If you are sharing something to look at or something to listen to, provided it is engaging, people will stop to watch or listen. The challenge is working within the limitations of Tumblr. Audio, for example, combined with a good cover image makes for great content. Our series, The Ministry of Peculiar Occurrences, has an award-winning podcast anthology, Tales from the Archives, and it gets coverage on Tumblr as well. However, in order to upload the content directly, the audio can be 10MB maximum and is limited to only once per day. Considering that the average short story we upload comes in at roughly 40 MB, it is not surprising that we have to remotely link such media. This material is said to be syndicated (a slightly different take on how you syndicate a blog post) back to Tumblr. When it comes to media, syndication allows for sharing of media beyond Tumblr's limitation.

Different social media has different demographics, and syndicating means you have the best chance of reaching all of them. It also can cut down on the amount of time you spend doing social media.

Avoiding a Potential Identity Crisis: Managing Accounts

You may have just one Tumblr account, but you can add up to ten secondary accounts a day, but each additional account comes with limitations. Your secondary accounts cannot follow other blogs, create questions, like, or submit posts. However, secondary blogs can be great if you want to have a main author page and different Tumblrs for your different series (if you have them). For an author, having too many Tumblr blogs—especially if you are spreading yourself over other social networks— can be a way to (pardon the pun) tumble down the rabbit hole. Having a main author blog as your primary blog and then secondary blogs for a new series or characters from new titles is more manageable.

If you ever get confused which of the primary and secondary blogs you are working on, click on the head icon in the top bar, and it will show you.

Tumblr Strategies

Tumblr is all about sharing in the moment. Make the most of a mobile app and share images, quotes from your work, book trailers, and reviews—this keeps your feed interesting and helps build your list of followers. Keep your smartphone handy and make those moments immediate. In doing so, you give your fans a peek behind the curtain. If you are at a convention or a book signing, then post those images, but try to keep them fun. Take pictures of your table, your readers and writers out on the town, or anything peculiar you find at the convention. If you find some interesting cosplay, excited readers with your books, or excited readers with you, post them!

Create a connection with your community by sharing memes, and news of interest to your readers. This can be about you or what is happening in the world around you.

As we've already said, video is popular on Tumblr, so if you have the time and skill to do it, then jump in. However, bear in mind that shorter is better, and that funny is even more engaging. You can record book reviews and chat about what is happening with your own writing and the challenges you are facing.

Repurpose your blog posts from WordPress to reach the Tumblr audience. Keep them short and pithy, and don't forget to include an image to catch their eye.

Quote sections from your book, and books you are reading, to build interest. When building an audience using book reviews, you will draw more viewers to your site by talking about books that are similar to yours. This is particularly useful when preparing to launch a book. Tease the heck out of your audience with riveting or intriguing snippets from your work. Make sure you don't reveal anything too important, though! The idea is to create cliff-hanger-type situations.

Since the Tumblr audience generally enjoys visuals, create images, videos, and GIFs to use. A riveting image combined with a pithy piece of text does a great job of drawing attention and interest.

If you're sharing audio or a podcast episode, be sure to include an attractive image that's associated with it. If you or your publisher are releasing an audiobook, use samples and post them online. Don't forget to include the links to where they can buy them.

Use the "Q&A" function to engage with your audience. If they don't ask you a question, post one yourself. Some questions might be about inspiration for your writing, why a character acted in a certain way, or perhaps plans for more books.

Remember: If you are using Tumblr as your secondary Web presence, include a link that leads back to your website in each post, so readers know where to go if they're looking for more content.

Between WordPress and Tumblr, the basics of blogging are well covered for you. Try one, or both, and get a feel of what works for you and where you think you will thrive. In the next chapter, we'll concentrate on ways to get your words and thoughts into your readers' ears. It's an exciting platform that delivers audio (and in some cases, videos) directly to computers and portable devices around the world, and it's a lot of fun!

III: FACEBOOK

THE KING OF SOCIAL MEDIA

I f social media was founded on blogging, then *Facebook* is what it has become. Sporting a membership of over 2.6 billion users, Facebook is the force of nature in social media that people hate to love and love to hate.

But what is it that makes Facebook (http://www.facebook.com) so appealing?

Before Facebook, social networking covered a wide variety of websites and applications. If you wanted to express an opinion and invite an audience to comment on your thoughts, you would blog. If you had photos you wanted to share, you would upload your photos to Flickr (http://flickr.com) and share links or embed your images in blog posts. If you wanted to swap a quick note with friends, you would use either AOL Instant Messenger, Yahoo! Messenger, or Skype. This meant hopping across multiple locations to share media, touch base with, and keep people in the know.

That all changed when Facebook brought to the Internet a one-stop website where photos could be uploaded and shared, thoughts in both long and short form could be posted, comments on these thoughts could be responded to with links, images, or both, and private messages could be shared with others online. With everything offered in one location, and how many users it has, it's easy to see how Facebook erupted in popularity and became the "necessary evil" in building your social media platform.

Setting Up a Facebook Account

Figure 3-1: Getting started on Facebook is easy and quick. A few details on your background, and you are underway.

STEP 1   Go to Facebook.com.

STEP 2   Fill in your name, email, password, date of birth, and gender.

 Make sure you use your proper author name so people can find you. Be aware Facebook's official rules say you should use your 'authentic name.' This has proved to be problematic with authors who use pen names or multiple names for different genres. Some authors choose to operate two profiles: one for their personal contacts and one as their professional. Others have a personal account from which they operate a Page as a professional author.

STEP 3   Single-click the "Sign Up" button.

STEP 4   You will be sent a code to the email, which you will need to add when prompted to confirm your account.

STEP 5   Upload your profile picture, find people you know and check out the privacy settings. Always a good thing to do.

Getting to Know Facebook

Facebook has many parts; it is, after all, one of the biggest and oldest social media platforms available. As you join and make Groups and Pages, it will get deeper; for now, let's look around this new platform. There is a lot to Facebook, but the first place to know intimately is the Navigation Bar, the nerve center of your personal account, pictured in Figure 3-2.

Figure 3-2: Facebook's navigation bar, your brand-new friend

From left to right, the Navigation bar is comprised of the following icons:

Facebook icon. This will bring you back to your main page

Search bar. Here you can look up people and Pages you might be interested in.

Home. Much like the Facebook icon, it will take you back to your main feed and Page.

Pages. This icon provides quick access to your Page.

Watch. Facebook will serve up the videos you've liked, and others they think you might.

Marketplace. Your local garage sale—for *gently used goods*, not where you want to post your book for sale.

Groups. All of the groups you manage and are part of.

Your Profile Icon. Clicking on this will take you to your profile timeline.

Create New Post (the "+" symbol). Single-click this to begin a new post.

Messages icon. Click on this icon of a speech bubble to review any private messages. Here you can also begin private conversations with other users from here.

Notifications icon. A bell icon, this Notifications tool is where all of your notifications will appear. For instance, if someone mentions your name in a post, you will be notified. Replies to your messages and posts, replies in Groups, and reactions earned from your posts all appear here.

Settings Drop-down Menu. This down arrow, on single-clicking it, accesses a detailed drop menu where you find Help services, Security options, and many other Facebook settings.

Setting Up a Group

Similar to the Navigation bar is your Shortcuts bar, located to the left of your Account and pictured in Figure 3-3. You find here a few quick links to Events along with Pages and Groups you follow. *Groups* are perhaps the most useful of Facebook's options when it comes to building a community, so let's set one up right now.

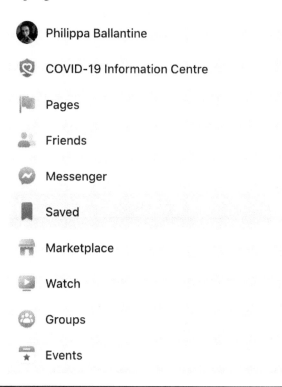

Figure 3-3: In your Shortcuts bar, you will find a series of quick links to your Events, Pages, and Groups.

Groups are communities built around a cause or common interest. Groups can be built for anything that people might have in common including a genre like science fiction and fantasy, Regency Romance, Steampunk, or D.I.Y. projects. The content appearing in Groups is community driven, and everyone shares a voice here.

STEP 1   Log into Facebook and click on the *Group* icon in the top bar.
STEP 2   Click on "+ Create New Group."
STEP 3   Upload an image that represents your Group.

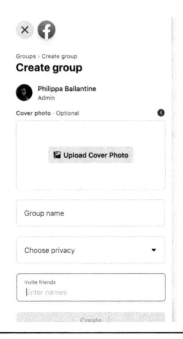

Figure 3-4: Setting up a Group only takes a few minutes.

STEP 4   Name your group.

STEP 5   Choose a Privacy setting.

           If this is a Group about your book, you will want this to be
           public.

STEP 6   Invite some Facebook friends into your Group (Optional).

When you are establishing your Group, Facebook encourages you to
draw from your own personal network in establishing its core membership.
Inviting people to your Group (or Page) is not a guarantee these Facebook
friends will join.

Completing Your Group's Profile

Now that your Group is live, you should go on and complete your
Profile. The Profile is how people find out about your Group; and that
this is a Group potential members of this community will want to join,
participate and support. A complete profile should answer the most basic
questions of any newcomers—primarily, *this is the place.*

STEP 1   Click on the *Group* icon in your header, and from there, select your Group.

STEP 2   On the left-hand side are your *Admin* tools. Scroll down and click on *Settings*.

STEP 3   Here you can change any of your Group settings. We suggest you customize the web address.

                You cannot change this once you get to 5,000 members, so sooner rather than later is a good idea.

STEP 4   Give your Group a brief description in the "Name and Description" field.

Figure 3-5: Within *Manage Group* settings, you can fine tune your group with details on what your Group is all about.

STEP 5   In *Manage Membership,* you set who can join your group, who approves member requests, and who is pre-approved to join. Since this is a group connected to your book, we suggest keeping membership to those who ask to join, to cut down on spammers.

                Never fear, all of these can be changed later as you come to grips with your Group.

Your Group is now complete, and up and running. All you need are members. So, on your next few posts that cross the line into business, mention that you have a Group and encourage people to join. Even before members join, have a few topics online and ready for discussion.

Starting a Group Topic Discussion

It's time to break the ice. Kick off a conversation with a simple discussion topic that can encourage your community to engage you (and others) in talking about something on your mind.

STEP 1   Go to your Facebook Group. At the top, just under the introduction banner, you should see a field that encourages "What's on your mind?"

STEP 2   Click in this field and write the following status message:

Welcome to my Facebook Group. This is where you will find all news and updates of my upcoming appearances and developments. The rules here are simple: don't spam and be excellent to one another. If you cannot do this, one of our moderators will promptly block you from the group. We hope you contribute and adhere to this positive spirit.

STEP 3   Click on the icon for Photo/Video if you wish to upload an accompanying photo. (If you wish to upload a different photo with your message or no photo at all, roll over the image and single-click the X in the top-right corner of the image.)

STEP 4   Click the "Post" button.

The most recent post in your group will appear at the top of your Group. This will always be the case until someone in the Group leaves a comment. The topic with the most recent comment will jump to the top of the feed, taking priority until a new topic is posted or another comment is left elsewhere in the various threads available in your Group.

Along with general discussions, you should note that you can upload photos and videos, ask questions of your Group members in poll fashion, or add a file (PDF, Word document, etc.) to share with your members. As a *moderator*, you can also decide what posts stay, what posts are deleted, and approve or dismiss members.

Setting up a Facebook Page

While a Group is a community that shares something in common and meets in one location to discuss it openly, a *Page* is very different in two respects. First, Pages come with an *Administrator's Control Panel* (or Admin Panel) that features built-in *analytics* (measurements of traffic coming to and from your Page, demographics, and performances of ad campaigns), options for *boosting posts* (paid advertisements), and options to *schedule posts* (you can either post immediately or set a later time for your message to appear in Facebook's *News Feeds*). Another difference between Pages and Groups is that moderators in Pages post as the *Page Host,* be it a business, a celebrity, or an organization. People who "Like" a Page can interact with page updates, but they themselves cannot post updates unless they are *Page Admins.* These are the posts appearing in News Feeds, regardless of whether you are following that page or not.

STEP 1   Go to your top bar, or to your left hand Shortcuts menu. Single-click on the Pages icon.

STEP 2   Click on "+ Create a New Page" to begin building your new Page.

Figure 3-6: Before launching, you will want to provide details and create a look for this new *Page* of yours.

STEP 3   Give the Page a name and select a category, as pictured in Figure 3-6.

   If it is for a book series, then "book" or "book series," or if it is for you as a professional then "writer" or "author." Put in a brief description, but don't worry too much—you will be able to change this later.

STEP 4   Click on "Create Page," and now you are off and running.

STEP 5   At the far-right of your Page's menu is the *Other Options* icon (three dots). Single-click this and select "Invite Friends" to begin building your audience (Optional).

 If you decide that a Facebook page is not working for your social media strategy, you can delete a Page by going onto the Page itself. Click on "Page Settings," located on the lower-left of your Page window. Under the "General" settings, at the very bottom of options listed here, you will find the "Remove Page > Delete Your Page" option. It's important not to leave unused platforms running. For more on this, see Chapter 11: Best Practices in Social Media.

Posting on a Page

Making a post on your Page is pretty easy, very similar to how you post in a Group. We're using in this exercise a previous post and blogpost we have posted on The Ministry of Peculiar Occurrences' page, so feel free to swap out our content with your own while following the steps provided.

STEP 1   Go to your Facebook Page. Just under the header, you should see a field with the words "Write a Post" visible. Click in this field.

STEP 2   Write the following status message:

Not all Kickstarter accounts succeed, as a Kickstarter is more than just crowdfunding. It is also a place for market testing and hard business lessons. (TM)

If you have more than one moderator for your Page, it is not a bad idea to end your post with initial signatures.

STEP 3   Hold down the "Shift" button and then hit "Return" twice. In this space, type here the following link: http://teemorris. com/2014/03/16/lessons-learned-kickstarter/

STEP 4   Once the link preview appears in the post, select the URL text and remove it. This is a nice way to clean up posts in order to avoid double posting a URL.

STEP 5   Click the "Post" button.

You've done it! Now let's dive deeper into the platform itself.

Facebook for Writers

We've set up a Group and a Page, but how can we as writers use them as a promotional platform? You may be approving connections with people you know only from a meeting at a convention or the purchase of a book, and this might be where the line blurs between personal and professional relationships on social media. Along with various strategies on how to leverage Facebook in your favor, we will talk about this line and how best to define it. Remember, Groups are a community built around a shared interest while Pages are more of a central hub of information where its host controls the signal, frequency, and variety of content. This means you may be stretching beyond your earlier "friend" definition.

Where Everybody Knows Your Name: Groups

One of the more recent advances in Facebook—and one we've been using a lot lately—is the ability to create a Group based around your Page—getting the best of both worlds. It means if you have enough of a following on your author page you can convert those followers into group members. We've built up a Ministry of Peculiar Occurrences page with thousands of followers, but to encourage interaction we have a group, Steampunk and the Ministry of Peculiar Occurrences. While we don't want just anyone posting on our main Page, within the Group we allow people to share their steampunk events, cosplaying, and constructions.

This way you can build an active, enthusiastic community around your work and your worlds, as the content featured on Groups is completely community driven. Everyone shares a voice in a Group, but since the discussion only happens when someone speaks up, it's a good idea to have a few topics ready for discussion before you invite readers or other authors to join. Having topics on hand also helps you avoid lulls in the Group's activity.

 You can kick off a Group by sending out invites to those who already like your Page. This will appear on the right-hand side of the Group. You won't be able to add everyone immediately, but you should be able to send between 30-40 invites per day.

As mentioned earlier, the most recent post made by a member will appear at the top of your Group until someone leaves a comment on a different post, restoring that topic to the top of the feed. When new content appears, you should take a moment to review it. As a Moderator, or people you assign in your Group as Moderators, you are Judge Dredd: judge, jury, and executioner. If you make your Group public, you decide who stays and who goes on account of bad behavior. With private groups, you also decide who is invited. Moderators must not only keep an eye on the behavior of its members and the approval of new ones, but also make certain members stay on topic. Gone unchecked, Groups can become havens for trolls (someone who is deliberately provocative, just to get a reaction) spambots, and people posting content completely inappropriate to your Group's topic. Moderation is paramount to keep your signal strong and the conversation of a high quality. Set ground rules for your Group and adhere to them. Like a garden, it can get out of control and full of weeds if you ignore it too long. Don't be afraid to mute or ban any members that stray too far outside the rules.

Groups are fantastic in creating a community; but if you are promoting a new release or even a short story in an upcoming anthology, your own post concerning your latest release may go missed if someone else posts a photo about seeing your previous book while in a bookstore or promoting their own project. With enough interaction, you can keep your post at the top of your Group's feed, but only until someone leaves a comment on a previous post. Once again, your promotion will be buried under previous posts.

Groups are better suited for communities established around a cause, an event, or a passion. Perhaps you want to host a writer's group—a safe place (provided you enforce your own guidelines) for writers of all skill levels and backgrounds to refine their storytelling talents? The focus with a Group like this should not be all on you, but you can easily claim your Group and its intent, a very subtle strategy of self-promotion if it becomes popular.

My House, My Rules: Pages

Similar to a Group, you want to make certain your Page and its profile is complete on launch. Remember that just as with a blog and a podcast, a Facebook Page should have all its information complete in order to make the best first impression that you can.

Your Page Profile Picture. While you have the option to rotate images in and out of visibility, this representation of you and your work should rarely change. If you are an author, this should be your current head shot or a custom logo designed for you and your books. If you create a Page for a series, it should be the most current cover or, as stated earlier, a custom logo that belongs to you. This is your brand, and when people see it at a glance, they should be able to easily connect this image with you or your business.

Your Cover Photo. Unlike a Profile Picture, your Cover Photo should rotate in and out for variety. The cover photo can display a number of things:

- Upcoming Events
- New Releases
- Upcoming Releases

You should find an image that serves as a "default" image (pertaining to your brand) but also take advantage of the Cover Photo as one of the promotion tools in your arsenal, seen in Figure 3-7.

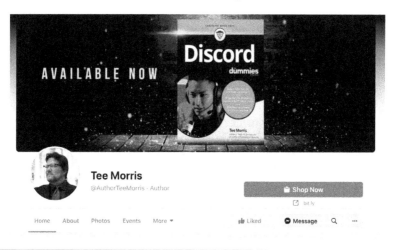

Figure 3-7: Your Author's Page can take advantage of the Cover Photo option, promoting your latest release or upcoming events.

About. Here is where you provide the details and contact information for your business and online connections.

Photos. The collection of photos you post to your Page.

Events. List of all the events you have coming up, as well as those from the past.

More. This is where you will find, Videos, and under Community, posts from those that have mentioned your Page.

The Like Option. When accessing your Page, you will know if you have *Liked this Page* or not. It's not vain to *Like* your own *Page*, as this is a way to monitor your own feed. Anything you share or post will appear in your personal feed, assuring you the Page's post is getting out.

Message. People can contact you from here.

Search. People can search your Page for keywords.

Shop Button. This is a link to take people to a shop where they can buy your book. We like to make sure ours are to our latest release.

Post. From this section of the Facebook Page, administrators can post status updates, links, announcements, photos and videos, and special events and milestones. These are the announcements that will appear on the *Updates Feed* of the Page.

Making a post on a Page is similar to making a post within a Group, with the exception of two points. First, your post will appear with the name of the Page, not your name, unless you select from a drop-down menu an option other than the Page's name. (This "posting option" menu is available in the Comments section, as well.) The other difference with posting on a Page is that updates will appear in the Page's Updates Feed in the order of posting, from the most recent at the top to older posts as you progress down the Page.

Now that we have an understanding of the differences between a Page and a Group, let's take a closer look at the difference in interaction. With Pages, the intent is to get shares and obtain reactions to your posts. To understand the why's behind this is to know this statistic — In 2020, there are approximately sixty million business Pages, but only six million are *active*.

What does that mean?

These active six million are building a presence, a personality, and a reputation on Facebook. Social Media is not simply throwing a switch and welcoming adoring fans to your corner of a network. Time and strategy achieve success in Facebook; and to do so, Pages post relevant content and pieces that are either based around your book, around your interests, or around topics relevant to your work.

So out of those six million active Pages, how do you get readers to Like your Page, provided they can find it?

"Go Like My Page" Posts. Probably the most common way to get your numbers up is by asking for Likes. Subtle ways of doing this include the use of print materials (business cards, postcards, etc.) that ask people to "Like us on Facebook." Restaurants, movies, bands, and all kinds of businesses employ this simple method. The more direct method is to compose a post that asks people to swing by your Page and Like it. Asking directly for Likes is not considered bad, provided this approach does not dominate your feed.

A once-a-week reminder, provided there is a variety of content in your feed, can serve as a polite, proactive approach to increasing your numbers.

Print Materials. When attending book events, you will see banners, flyers, postcards, and even business cards, all featuring an author's website, e-mail, and maybe even a Twitter account in lieu of a phone number. If you can find a place to promote your Page, either on the back cover or in the interior front matter of your books, make it happen. If you're going to promote a Facebook Page in print, it is paramount to have a URL that's easy for people to remember and easy to read in print, like facebook.com/TheMinistryOfPeculiarOccurrences which neatly fits on a business card.

Boosting Posts and Pages. Facebook periodically changes its algorithms for News Feeds so that previously Liked pages no longer appeared automatically in your feed. In order to Boost a Post or Page, you have to pay Facebook a fee. In turn, it promotes the signal of a single post or the entire Page. Doing so can make a huge difference in your reach, at least according to the analytics.

But are people actually seeing your advertisements or simply scrolling past them in order to get to that cute kitten picture? Between boosting individual posts or Pages, we have found that boosting individual posts is a smarter tactic. Not every post, mind you, as that would smell a bit of SPAM. (And let's be honest, you don't want your page to reek of the scent of SPAM.) Promoted posts should cover key topics worth your money:

- New book releases
- Exclusive events
- Award announcements

It is up to you to decide if boosting a post is worth the financial investment, but be smart about where your money goes with Facebook. Most writers have a limited budget and therefore must be careful about where they invest. Think about where you really want to direct your reader's eyeballs.

Telling Stories on Facebook

Inspired by Snapchat and Instagram (which Facebook purchased in 2012), *Facebook Stories* are short videos or images which are a quick way to connect with your audience. You can only do Stories on your mobile device. By clicking on "Create a story" you get options of the kinds of files to upload. You can either pick a picture off your phone or take one with your phone. Then you can add text, effects, stickers, and tag people. Boomerangs, a short-looped video, can also be done with Stories.

So why aren't more authors creating Stories? Stories disappear after 24 hours.

Stories are great for momentary parts of your author life. Sharing events your attending, for example, is a great way to spread the experience you are having right now. We've seen some neat Boomerangs from book signings for example. However, if you want to have something about your book that remains in place, a post on your Page or in your Group would be better. That information remains in place for readers to refer to. If you want to find out more about Stories, check in our Instagram chapter where we go more in depth, since this is where people are more inclined to look at them.

Lights, Camera, Action: Facebook Live

In 2016 Facebook started offering *Facebook Live,* an instant, authentic way to reach your audience through video. This incredibly spontaneous, live approach to social media has brought many authors success in connecting with their readers. It can be done from both computers and mobile devices, so you can go live from your Page (what we recommend) provided you have a strong enough Internet connection.

Two particular authors are shining examples of mastering this intimate look at an author's lifestyle. Mary Katherine Backstrom, writer of Mom Babble: The Messy Truth About Motherhood, is known for her honest and frequent chats about everyday occurrences and disasters. Her laughter and genuine kindness have brought her thousands of fans, including The Ellen Show who couldn't get enough of her Facebook Live check-in's. Then there's New York Times bestseller Gail Carriger, best known for her Parasol Protectorate and Custard Protocol series, hosting events on Facebook Live where she answers questions, shares previews of upcoming releases, and makes announcements as to where she will be.

The only qualifier we would add, is that Facebook Live, is… well… *live.* Be aware that whatever you put out there during these events, stays out there.

A few tips, once you are aware of that:

Give your Live a compelling description to encourage people to watch. Decide if you want to tag friends and locations. Again, think of privacy and safety when you do this.

Steer away from the fun filters. They are fun for personal use but distracting if you are trying to give off an air of professionalism.

Be aware of the background behind you. No one literally wants to see your dirty laundry.

When you start a Live, don't launch straight into your important information. Chat a bit to allow people to get the notification that you are on, and tune into your stream.

Wear something tidy or professional. If you're a steampunk author, that could mean the latest fashion in brass and rivets.

For more on how to make the most of Facebook Live, take a look at Chapter 8 which goes into more detail on how to turn your writing nook into a proper streaming studio.

There is a lot to Facebook, and there is a lot not to like about the platform. Can you afford to cut it out of your promotional routine? Nothing comes close to the reach of Facebook, but while you continue to test the platform's limits, keep in mind you have other options in social media. Facebook, powerful as it is, should not be your one and only spot. Your audience, you may discover in working with social media, may not be on Facebook. Keep your mind and options open, and explore what other platforms have to offer.

IV: TWITTER

BREVITY IS THE SOUL OF WIT

When it comes to a user-friendly interface and a true plug-and-play spirit, it rarely comes as easy as *Twitter* (http://www.twitter.com), launched in 2006 by developers Jack Dorsey, Evan Williams, Biz Stone and Noah Glass. The service has gone through different stages of use, popularity, and application. In the early days, the social networking site was a terrific tool to stay in touch and communicate with friends. In a matter of a few years, Twitter found itself rife with self-anointed social media gurus passing along inspirational quotes, needless spam of all varieties, and regurgitation of tweets from other accounts.

We refer to that period of Twitter's lifespan as *The Dark Times.*

Twitter has gone through various renaissances since its launch over a decade ago. For many writers, Twitter is an extension for other popular networks like LinkedIn, Pinterest, and Instagram. For other writers, Twitter still serves as a reliable, trusted mobile communication option, regarded as one of the cornerstones within a strong social media platform. Twitter is many things to many people, and Twitter for an author should be:

- A connection with other authors, both for professional networking and for finding new and unique resources for their work
- A promotional platform for works currently in print or digital formats, and for special offers concerning their works

- A direct line of communication to your fans, making their day with a quick reply

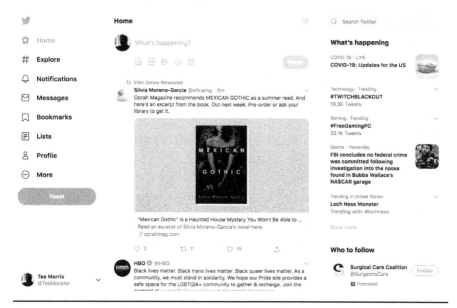

Figure 4-1: Twitter (https://twitter.com) is considered one of the "must have's" in a writer's social media plan.

The Deets with the Tweets: Setting Up Twitter

Twitter is easy to get right, but it can be nightmare for you and your followers if you get it wrong. If you have not set up an account yet, let's get you set up.

STEP 1 Go to https://twitter.com on your browser.

STEP 2 Click the "Sign Up" button, and enter in your name, a phone call or email, and a date of birth. Once the fields are complete, single-click the "Next" button.

Keep your Name/Username on brand as much as possible. If you have "Tee Morris" for example as your main username throughout your social media accounts, try to stay close to that instead of using variations like "T Morris" or "Thomas Morris" which could create confusion.

STEP 3   In the next step, you can decide if Twitter can keep track of your activity in order to customize your experience on the platform. Once you grant or deny permission, click the "Next" button.

STEP 4   Review what you have offered for your Twitter credentials and single-click the "Sign Up" button.

You are immediately taken to what will eventually become your Twitter homepage. There will be an explanation of what a tweet is and how it will appear in your Twitter stream.

STEP 5   You will be sent a verification code. Enter in the code and then single-click the "Next" button.

STEP 6   For the profile picture and bio, single-click the "Skip this Step" option as we will be covering these options later in this chapter.

STEP 7   From the list of interests offered, single click as many interests you like. You can also use the "Search" field to enter in interests related to writing.

STEP 8   Select which Twitter account you would like to follow straight away. When done, single-click the "Next" button.

These Twitter accounts are featured accounts of high-profile, verified accounts. You can tweet to them; but the likelihood of earning a reply, while possible, is unlikely.

Your Twitter account is now live, and you are ready to reach out and start interacting with people. However, we recommend before you send out a *tweet* (the official name of a post, reply or update on Twitter) to finish up our user profile as we want to make the best of first impressions.

If people were to visit your Twitter page, do you have a profile picture that introduces you to potential followers? Does this profile picture represent how you want to be perceived online? How about the header photo stretching across the top of the page? Is there something there that completes your profile page? What does your bio say about you? Is it complete? Is it snarky?

All these details are part of the first impression that you and your Twitter account make on new visitors.

An Author's Profile Photo: Worth a 1000 Tweets

The profile picture can be regarded the same as when you are making an appearance at a bookstore, a convention, or a writing festival. The author who shows up to a panel discussion prepared for the topic at hand

and presenting themselves in a professional manner will be regarded very differently than the writer who has not bothered to prepare for the topic and looks as if they couldn't bother to brush their hair or find something better to wear than an "I Love Books" tee-shirt. The photo you use as your profile becomes part of your personal brand, representing who you are and what you do.

Tee Morris
@TeeMonster

Writer of The Ministry of Peculiar Occurrences from Harper Voyager, Ace Books, and Imagine That! Studios. Writer of "For Dummies" books. discord.gg/ss9w

◎ Manassas, Virginia, USA ⦿ twitch.tv/theteemonster ▦ Joined July 2007

8,723 Following **8,395** Followers

Figure 4-2: A profile picture, along with banner art and a completed bio, helps put your best foot forward on Twitter.

Profile pictures should be:

- around 700K in file size
- 400 x 400 pixels in dimension, recommended (Twitter offers you cropping options.)
- A resolution of 72 pixels per inch (ppi)
- Saved as JPEG or PNG formats, in an RGB color scale

Before you start tweeting, your priority is to find a profile picture that best represents you. Does the picture you currently have posted or you're considering to use as your profile picture make the professional impression you want to make? Does your brand have a sense of humor, or is it more polished? Camera phones and simple photo editors make profile pictures a breeze, but what should you use and what should you avoid? What are your options?

Option One: A Picture of You

Perhaps the simplest and best way to introduce yourself to people is to use a photo of yourself. A picture of you gives a face to put with the Twitter handle, a more personal connection you are making with people. Depending on your creativity, this kind of profile picture can also work on reflecting your particular mood that day.

Before you use your smartphone of choice and take a quick selfie of yourself or you run out to find that wicked-awesome photo of you in a tuxedo or evening dress, consider this approach:

- Use pictures taken either from the chest or neck up. Remember that those using Twitter applications, especially ones on smartphones, will be looking at small profile pictures. Full body shots of you will be imperceptible. Keep your photo tightly cropped and close up.
- Avoid images with busy backgrounds. What is happening behind you is just as important as how you look. Too much detail or activity in the background (what some photographers refer to as noise) can make profile pictures on Twitter difficult to make out. Keep what's happening behind you to the basics.
- Avoid offensive imagery. This could provide a challenge for horror and erotica authors, and an additional challenge in what is deemed "offensive" as "offensive" is subjective. Use your best judgment. No nudity. Refrain from obscene gestures. Keep gore level to the barest of minimums.

Option Two: Using a Personal Logo

Branding, which you've seen referenced throughout this book, has been associated in the past with business, public relations, and marketing strategies. Today, with the modern author shouldering the majority of book promotion whether published by New York or their own publishing line, this concept is no longer reserved for advertising agencies to pitch and charge corporate entities top dollar. Authors are now taking to heart principles of branding and applying it to their social media platforms.

A simplified definition of branding is an approach to your business through association with a word, catch phrase, or an image. You see it everywhere. Two golden arches usually mean a McDonalds is within sight. A stylized arrowhead worn just over the left breast might make you think of *Star Trek*. A chubby, blue bird taking flight, and we're talking about Twitter. If you have a product or a service that people associate with a phrase, name, or some other identifier, that is successful, effective branding.

Much like with using a self-portrait as your profile picture, creating a brand for yourself offers its unique set of challenges.

- Make sure your logo is original, and your own. You might think this is common sense, but whether it is authors who parody corporate giants or make their own logo a variation on another's theme, it is best to come up with something original. Make it your own. Make it unique.
- Avoid text-heavy or busy images as personal logos. Keep it simple. If your self-designed or professionally-commissioned logo comes with tag lines, pen names, or URL's, accept that this will be lost when it is rendered in a space smaller than 75 x 75 pixels. For our multimedia studio, Imagine That!, our brand is a stylized double koru. Remember: the busier you make it, the harder it will be to recognize it at a glance. Logo designs are best when basic.
- Branding does not happen overnight. Use your logo beyond Twitter and give yourself time for brand recognition. When we release our books or book trailers under the Imagine That! banner, we make sure the logo is visible. Use your logo consistently and constantly in your promotional materials, and beyond social media, building brand recognition for yourself.

Option Three: Using Interests, Hobbies, or Something Out-of-the-Ordinary

For the I-really-hate-to-be-photographed or the I-really-have-zero-artistic-ability authors, there is a final option. From zombified George Washington to a variety of characters from video games (both of the 8-bit days and the modern *Destiny* resolutions), profile pictures that reflect your interests are still an option. What do these images do for you in the way of branding? Absolutely nothing. What about making a connection with your network? Maybe, provided you continue to talk about that particular interest. The people following your network may not even know about your writing career unless you mention it in your biography though.

If, however, you would rather keep a distance between your network and your own likeness—not uncommon for authors—then this option maintains a sense of privacy for the concerned author. The profile picture can even serve as "mood indicators" if you do not necessarily commit yourself to one particular profile picture. When your Twitter picture is of Full Metal Jacket's R. Lee Emery giving "good drill sergeant" or William Shatner screaming into a communicator, people know you're having a bad day. Then you have Figure 4-3 of Pip's latest profile picture—her D&D character, Ashimei, and pet dinosaur, George.

The problem with swapping out avatars is the loss of brand recognition. As mentioned earlier, branding works through repetition of an image so that consumers associate you or your company with it. If you want to take advantage of that recognition, keep your profile picture consistent.

Philippa Ballantine
@PhilippaJane Follows you

Figure 4-3: Sometimes, a profile picture can be a celebration of your interests outside of writing, like Pip's own D&D pursuits. (Original artwork by Candy Cane Studios)

Of course, there are exceptions to this advice, and there are ways to continue branding while swapping out profile pictures. Imagine That! Studios, during the Christmas holidays, uses an image of a stocking cap draped across a computer with the double koru logo in plain view. Pip's "Ashimei & George" profile pic is on Twitter . . . along with Facebook, Tumblr, and elsewhere. Be smart about how you swap out profile pictures. Decide on a strategy and be consistent with the image you are portraying.

Now that you have a profile photo in place, let's take a closer look at the header photo for the profile page.

The Header Photo: Setting a Tone on Twitter

Similar to the Facebook cover photo which also incorporates a banner-style photo option on both personal profiles and Pages, the header photo is a space where you can add in a favorite horizontal photo as set dressing for your profile. If the profile photo is your first impression, the header photo is your stage, offering either an atmosphere or a tone for this Twitter account.

Header photos are much like their Profile counterparts with a few differences here and there:

- 5MB (maximum) in file size
- 1500 x 1500 pixels in dimension, recommended (Twitter offers you cropping and positioning options.)
- Measure 72 pixels per inch (ppi) in resolution
- Saved as JPEG or PNG formats, in an RGB color scale

The header photo is a small detail, but another place to express yourself and your interests. Header photos can also change when you feel change is needed. Author's discretion.

- Make sure header photos are landscape. In the case of Twitter's header photo, you need to think horizontally instead of vertically. Wide, panoramic shots work best.

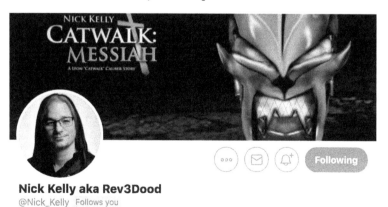

Nick Kelly aka Rev3Dood
@Nick_Kelly Follows you

Figure 4-4: The header photo, by being landscape in orientation, allows for proper spacing between the image (in this case, Nick Kelly's cover art from his cyberpunk series, *Catwalk*) and the profile picture.

- Be as creative and as expressive as you will. The profile photo is how people identify you, but the header photo can really be about you, your interests, and your passions. As a writer, it can be of your favorite place to write, a stock photo of a library, or a (horizontal) portion of a book cover as seen in Figure 4-4. This is you setting a mood for your Twitter profile. Have some fun.

- Design header photos using Rule of Thirds within the 1500 x 1500 dimensions. Some header photos on other pages may appear jagged, out-of-focused, or distorted. This is caused by Twitter attempting to fill the header region with an image too small or at a ratio where distortion happens. Experiment with image sizes, or design using horizontal thirds on a 1500 x 1500 canvas. Visit http://en.wikipedia.org/wiki/Rule_of_thirds for a detailed explanation and design tips.

- Make sure to take into account how the header photo will be seen on both the computer screen and the mobile app. Templates are available online to help you put the important part of the image in the part of the screen that will be seen by both.

What goes into a header photo is strictly up to you. As an author, it is not a bad idea to change the header photo to include a portion of your latest cover release, provided it isn't too busy. For the more ambitious author possessing a mastery of Photoshop or some other photo editor, designing a banner promoting an upcoming event or release would work great in promoting what you have coming up in the way of appearances. People will see this backdrop when they follow notifications directly to your profile, check out your details on their smartphone, and see it on other Twitter clients.

Now that we have a look for our profile, let's perfect that final touch.

The Bio: Making an Introduction

It astounds us how many authors left this blank or slap on a link to their books without any thought. (More on that in a moment.) The bio, even within the limitations of 160 characters, is an opportunity to introduce yourself.

Much like with profile and header photos, authors employ several ways of introducing themselves in their bios:

The Professional Approach: "#1 New York Times bestselling author. Master knitter. Bassist for Evan Diamond. • Free, weekly fiction podcast at http://scottsigler.com/subscribe." (Scott Sigler, @scottsigler) and "Hugo and Astounding winner, Podcaster HoF. SOLO, SIX WAKES, DITCH DIGGERS, ESCAPE POD, ISBW -She/Her-." (Mur Laffery, @mightymur)

The Snarky Approach: "Reeling and Writhing" (Harper Voyager author Mary Victoria, @MAdamsVictoria), "I enjoy pie." (Hugo-winning author John Scalzi, @scalzi)

Somewhere In Between: "Author of the bestselling True Heroes series. Foodie. Frequent Flyer. Day Job Road Warrior. Alter-identity: PJ Schnyder." (Piper J Drake, @piperjdrake), "Kiwi word herder, cat butler, and collaborating creative. Somewhat responsible for Books of the Order, Shifted World, and Ministry of Peculiar Occurrences." (Philippa Ballantine, @philippajane)

- Write a bio that is not overloaded with links. There are authors that use their bios to get in Facebook links, Instagram links, and others. Keep it simple and write a bio that means something. Leave the URL for the URL field underneath the bio and location field.
- Much like the header photo, be as creative as you can. You can express your love of pie, a quote that motivates you to write, or express your excitement for a debut novel coming soon. Your bio should be sincere, succinct, and a summary of what you are all about.
- Make your location as close as you can. It can be as simple as the largest city closest to you, the coast of the country where you are located, but let people know where you are in the world, or even in a state of mind, if inclined.
- Have your URL go to your main site or blog. A strategy of social media repeated often in this guide is guiding traffic from social networks to your website. The final destination of your network should not be a platform like Twitter or Facebook. The destination should be your website, the corner of the Internet that has everything a reader would find about you, your works, and where you will be appearing next.

Let's say at the end of this book, you have a **LOT** of platforms you want to share with people. And let's say you didn't want your Twitter to be an onslaught of links. This is why you want to set yourself up on Link Tree (https://linktr.ee/), a third-party service that offers all of your links at one location. Whether you use the free or Pro option, Link Tree takes all your URLs and helps you organize them. Now, anyone who clicks on a link like https://linktr.ee/theteemonster will now be able to find you wherever you have set up a profile.

With a breakdown of the profile's three sections, we can now complete our own.

STEP 1   Go to http://twitter.com on your browser while logged in. Click on the "Profile" option, located in the left-hand menu.

STEP 2   Click the "Edit Profile" button to access your Profile options.

STEP 3   In the circle featuring the blank silhouette, single-click the camera icon and find a picture that best works for you as a profile picture.

STEP 4   Once you find your picture, select it and single-click the "Choose" button.

                    If you need to adjust the photo, Twitter will offer you those options.

STEP 5   In the rectangle featuring a blank space, single-click the camera icon and find a picture that best works for you as a header photo.

STEP 6   Once you find your picture, select it and single-click the "Choose" button.

                    If you need to adjust the photo, Twitter will offer you those options.

STEP 7   In the "Bio" section, create your 160-character log bio. Keep an eye at the lower-right corner of your bio, as seen in Figure 4-5, to see how close you are coming to the limit.

Figure 4-5: Before you set to tweeting, make sure your profile is complete and ready for the world.

STEP 8   Scroll down, if needed, and enter in your location, if desired.

STEP 9   Scroll down, if needed, and enter in a website you wish to point people to for more information.

STEP 10   Scroll down, if needed, and enter in your birthday, if desired.

Following this profile audit, your first impression should be polished and ready for welcoming and connecting with new readers, fans of your works, and other authors. It's now time to tweet what's on your mind, or what you are working on.

But what do you say? Is anyone really listening? And how do you really say anything intelligent within 280 characters?

It is now time to embrace your inner editor and get over the fear of brevity. As Shakespeare once said, it's the soul of wit.

Mastering Tweet Speak

All communication on Twitter begins with the statement you type into the message field, or what Twitter refers to as a tweet. When we introduce beginners, we still get the furrowed brow or the eyeroll at the cutesy-cutesy name used for Twitter's updates. And we reply with the same truth: Yes, it's called a tweet. You're using Twitter. Get over it.

The biggest pushback from authors continues to be the concern about the 280-characters-or-less limitation. You can't say a lot in that limited platform, right?

Actually, there is a lot you can say on Twitter. You have to be smart and strategic about what you say, how you say it, and how to edit a detailed, in-depth post down to the essentials. There is a science to putting a tweet together. To do this means understanding and mastering an economy of words.

Let's say you want your first tweet to be:

> I'm awake this morning and waiting for the coffee to brew. I've got a big day ahead of me with edits, rewrites, and proposals all screaming for my attention. Oh yeah, and I've got an audiobook to get together for Audible. Yes, it looks a little overwhelming, but I'm feeling confident and ready to rock!

There are just over 304 characters (and that includes spaces) in this statement. The main points of this tweet are:

- You're awake.
- The coffee is brewing.
- Your To Do list is very full for the day.
    - edits
    - rewrites
    - proposals
    - an audiobook for Audible
- You're feeling overwhelmed by it all.
- You're confidence level is high and you're ready to accomplish all the things!

You want to say all this, but this update could easily take up two tweets. We should try to get this down to one tweet, and have it look like this:

> Coffee brews as edits, rewrites, and proposals await. Kicking off the day with an @ACX_com submission. Let's make it happen. #determined

300 characters has now been pruned down to 136 characters after making logical edits:

- You're tweeting, so no need to let us all know you're awake.
- It's also clear you've got a big day ahead as you've got "edits, rewrites, and proposals" needing attention.
- If you want to highlight the Audible project, tell your network you're "Kicking off the day with an @ACX_com submission." Mentioning Audible by using their handle

can attract their attention, maybe even start up an exchange.

- If you're feeling confident and ready to rock, sum it up in one affirmation.
- At this point you have plenty of room for more. You can implement an image or a hashtag in case you want to track the conversation. So, we have added #determined into our tweet.

So, hold up — what's a Hashtag?

Hashtags are tracking tools that allow you to identify tweets and other postings under a quick-to-find category in any search engine or platform-specific search. The origins of a hashtag could conceivably be traced back to 1970 when hash symbols highlighted items in IT programming. It then evolved into a form of identification for groups and topics on Internet Relay Chat (IRC) networks and still does so in communication tools like Discord and Slack. The hashtag first appeared on Twitter on August 23, 2007, when Chris Messina tweeted "How do you feel about using # (pound) for groups. As in #barcamp [msg]?"

Yes, the first tweet to use a hashtag was about hashtags.

Hashtags are the best way to track a conversation on Twitter. Whether you are using the "Search Twitter" options on the website or official Twitter app, or if you have created a dedicated column in TweetDeck (https://tweetdeck.com), hashtags allow you to follow a conversation, provided participants consistently use it in the conversation, and the hashtag being used is the same hashtag. When creating an official hashtag for an event, you want to keep it easy to remember and as few characters as possible. For example, instead of a podcast or a special event centered around the Ministry of Peculiar Occurrences, the hashtag would not be #MinistryOfPeculiarOccurrences but #MoPO instead.

Not all tweets need hashtags, but there are times and events on Twitter when hashtags are essential. Observe how hashtags are utilized, and when you are attending events, always ask if there is an official hashtag so that your tweets can be found easily with the event's official channels.

With a tweet put together — and this might feel like a laborious process, but the more you do it, the easier it will be for you to put together a tweet — we can go on and post our first tweet.

STEP 1   Go to https://twitter.com on your Internet browser. If you are logged in and you told Twitter to remember you, you should still be logged in. (If not, go ahead and log back into Twitter.)

STEP 2   Single-click the "Tweet" button on your Twitter homepage.

STEP 3   In the "Compose" window, offered in the left-hand sidebar, enter in the following:

Hi, everyone! This is my first tweet. Thanks for the help on this, @ TeeMonster and @PhilippaJane. #SM4W #WelcomeToTwitter

Tweets should be checked for typos and grammar as there is no editing a tweet once it goes live.

STEP 4   Single-click the "GIF" icon located at the bottom of the tweet composition window, as seen in Figure 4-6. In the search bar above the GIF menu, type in "Hi" and single-click a GIF you want to use for your tweet.

Tweets with graphics, GIFs, and video clips tend to earn more traffic than text-based only tweets. Make sure the media attached with your tweet is relevant to the actual tweet itself.

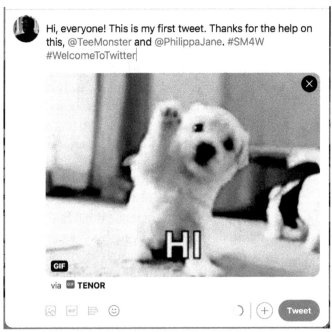

Figure 4-6: Tweets with GIFs, images, and video added see a sharp increase in traffic.

STEP 5   Single-click on the "Tweet" button.

Type. Proof. Post. That's all there is to it! Your message is now out in the Twitterverse for those in your network and the Public Timeline to see.

The really cool thing about Twitter, though, is not the ability to get your thoughts out and broadcast to a larger group of people, but you can also respond to tweets and connect with other people around the world.

Replying to a Tweet

Let's take a look at how an exchange can go on Twitter. A back-and-forth conversation with someone.

At the time of this writing, Tee hosted a charity stream for the organization, No Kid Hungry (https://twitter.com/nokidhungry). He posted a tweet, pictured in Figure 4-7, letting people know about the stream and the link where people could donate. Along with the URLs to his stream and to the donation link, No Kid Hungry was tagged (the equivalent of a "shout-out" in social media where another person is mentioned in a posting) in the tweet.

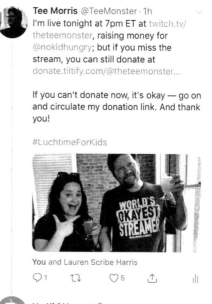

Figure 4-7: Conversations on Twitter are rendered in threads where the top tweet is the most recent tweet, or the beginning of the conversation.

A few minutes later, a tweet arrived in Tee's feed:

No Kid Hungry / @nokidhungry
Replying to @TeeMonster and @LaurenScribe
adds to calendar Thanks, Tee!

This is how a reply appears in Twitter, a tweet featuring a user's name and avatar, the usernames included in the reply, and finally the tweet itself. Replying to a tweet is important as it is an indication you are paying attention to your Twitter stream, and replies can lead to some really important connections.

They can also lead to some incredibly fun exchanges.

STEP 1   When a reply arrives in your Mentions stream, single-click on the speech bubble, located to the left of the four options underneath your tweet.

STEP 2   Enter in your reply in the tweet composition window.

STEP 3   Single-click the "Reply" button.

Twitter notifies you that your reply is sent. And there you go. Just like that, you're having a conversation on Twitter.

Another form of replying is called the *retweet*. How a retweet works is, through a single click, you copy another Twitter account's tweet or reply.

STEP 1   In your "Home" Timeline window, find a tweet you want to share with your network. Single-click on the looping arrows —the "Retweet" option—and either retweet or retweet with a comment from you.

As seen in Figure 4-8, retweets can either be sent as the tweet itself or a retweet with comment. The second option, retweet with comment, gives you an opportunity to add your own thoughts about what you are retweeting.

STEP 2   Single-click the "Retweet" button.

Retweets are terrific methods in spreading a message, a link, or just something really cool throughout your network. If you're lucky, your retweet will be picked up by others. The retweet is instrumental in a tweet going viral.

Figure 4-8: Content can be easily shared on Twitter by using the Retweet feature. You can either retweet the content or share the retweet with your own thoughts attached to it.

What to Do on Twitter

Establishing and evaluating a presence on Twitter is not simply based on the amount of followers or the frequency of when you tweet. There are a multitude of Twitter accounts currently live; and many, many authors tweet the good, the bad, and the downright ugly. What you should strive for is a Twitter feed that offer content relevant to you, your interests, and the books you write.

The first thing authors should do before the book comes out is to launch your Twitter account. Begin building your platform in order to become part of the community. You do this by talking about what interests you and find out what interests those following you. Delve into what you're binging on Netflix, Amazon, or elsewhere. Share a few thoughts on the last movie you saw, or last book you read (provided it's a positive review). Post images of where you're traveling. Twitter, along with many other social media platforms, is about community and interaction. Keep your feed interesting and lively by talking about things other than your book. People want to get to know you. It is your choice how much you want to share, and you should set boundaries for yourself; but talking about your book and only your book will get very old very quick.

Aim for one *"buy my book"* tweet within every five-to-ten tweets. Show people you're wanting to connect and communicate with them instead of constantly selling something.

While building your network and tweeting with others, seek out and follow other writers, publishers, and agents. Before following them, however, review their feeds. See if they are actually having conversations with people, or simply talking at their networks. Twitter feeds of professionals serve as a great way to listen in on what is happening in the marketplace, depending on the quality of their conversations. A solid Twitter feed can also keep you in the know on which agents are looking for new clients, what publishers are seeking from the slush pile, or provided advance warning on publishing scams.

Screening Twitter feeds is a great way to assure your network is built on quality as opposed to quantity. Sure, there are writers who sport tens of thousands or even hundreds of thousands of followers, but how well are they actually connecting with their networks. What is the worth of a Twitter feed that is nothing but constant retweets, posting of famous quotes, and incessant *"Buy My Book Now!!!"* links. Check out each person who follows you, and only follow back those that are actually people. You may find your numbers will climb much slower, and you may never crack the "10,000 Followers" mark. You will, however, have a Twitter network that is responsive, receptive, and reliable.

Another strategy in building a responsive, receptive, and reliable network, a priority in your Twitter feed should be to reply to mentions. When a mention comes in, provided it is coming from a real, bona fide person and not a spambot, tweet a reply. This is how communication begins and you never know which communication will lead to a new reader. Guaranteed though—you will make that person's day with a simple *"Thank you for reading my book."* tweet.

What NOT to do on Twitter

It takes patience in building a quality network, but you cannot torpedo a Twitter account with the occasional slip-up. (No one is perfect. Twitter is proof of that.) Continuously bad behavior and thoughtless actions, however, can severely undermine whatever sense of community you're trying to establish on Twitter.

The biggest, most common mistake authors make on Twitter is turning their account into one giant infomercial about their book. You have seen them when they follow you. Every tweet—*every single tweet*—is a link to their book, sometimes ten to twenty tweets in a day. (That's not an exaggeration. We've seen it.) They may be written in such a fashion where Twitter will not automatically flag them for spam, but a constant stream of links to your book and how scary-awesome it is fails to build a community around you or your book. If your Twitter stream is one self-promotional post after another, your best case scenario is you will not receive a reciprocal follow back. Worst case—you will get reported for SPAM.

The second most common mistake authors make on Twitter is beg for followers on Twitter. You may receive a mention thanking you for the follow, immediately followed by a request for you to like their Facebook page. The worst is when you receive an automatic Direct Message asking you for a Like. Desperation isn't attractive in any situation, and makes you look unprofessional. Get to know your network on Twitter as it will be a very different network from Facebook or Instagram. If those Twitter followers who visit other platforms like what you have to say, they will find you on your blog, Facebook, or elsewhere. Trolling for followers is just tacky.

Equally tacky tactics include:

- Misrepresenting yourself in your bio. (We once had a writer follow us who described themselves in their bio as a bestselling author…and their debut novel was coming out later that year.)
- Filling your Twitter feed with inspirational quotes from other books and authors. People follow you to hear what you have to say, not revel in the wisdom of others.
- Filling your Twitter feed with inspirational quotes from your own books and you yourself. Yes, people want to know what's on your mind, but you're not that important. Keep yourself in check.
- Filling your Twitter feed with nothing but retweets. Retweeting is not participation or engagement. It can be part of it, but only retweeting others is regurgitation.
- Following people only to drop them later in the same day. Many third-party applications and services who promise you more followers will follow other Twitter accounts. Once the followed reciprocates, they are immediately dropped off your feed. This is a tactic on the wrong side of ethical.

Authors behaving badly on Twitter come in many forms, but it is a good idea to practice the same etiquette you would practice in the real world. For example, pitching ideas to agents and editors upon meeting them. Would you, at an event, walk up to an agent or editor and say, "I have an idea you must look at!" without introducing yourself or ever asking if the agent or editor is accepting pitches? Probably not, but it happens on Twitter. Often. Get to know these professionals as both pros and as people. Find out who is looking and what they want. Never pitch to editors or agents online unless asked.

On applying these basic approaches and strategies to your profile — the way you compose tweets, how you approach hashtags, working to avoid the pitfalls many authors tend to find for themselves — Twitter becomes a very different platform. What should happen from this point is investing time into developing your presence and your community. Get comfortable with Twitter and apply these positive methods. Watch how the interaction between you and your network improves. All that remains now is building on your reputation and changing your Twitter account from a promotional platform to a community, a community that doubles as a team of promoters dedicated to the success of your works.

V: INSTAGRAM

ADDING PHOTOGRAPHY TO YOUR ARSENAL

Facebook and Twitter all offer the ability to post photos as part of your updates, and people still take advantage of this option. You may have noticed, in the past two years or so, that your social networks—particularly in their mobile versions—have been offering a variety of filters for your photographs. One filter might make your image appear like an antique image from the 19th century. Another filter may give your image the look of a Polaroid One-Step from the 1970's.

What? You don't know what a One-Step is? Look it up on the Internet. And *get off my lawn!*

These creative options possibly came about on account of an unassuming app that took photographs from your smartphone's camera and added to the moment a nostalgic look. Launched in October 2010 and sporting over one billion active users monthly, Instagram (http://instagram.com) took online photography in a backwards direction, granting its users the ability to take pristine, megapixel photos and turn them into 1970's-tastic, antique, or cinematic photographs. You can add slick borders, quirky angles, and a variety of color effects to your photos, as well as tag your location (using a process commonly known as geotagging) and other Instagram members into your images.

In 2013 Instagram added the ability to post videos. Presently, Instagram allows you to post up to a minute of video from your smartphone to your *Feed,* the various photos and video clips you receive from other people you are following. Outside of your Instagram Feed, you also have access to Instagram *Stories,* temporary posts that feature looped animations, quick video clips, or notifications of what you're doing or where you are currently. You can either make it a single, continuous 15-second shot, or put together a series of segments. Finally, there is *IGTV.* Any video longer than one minute of running time appears here. In its decade online, Instagram has grown and evolved into a multi-platform app where some writers focus on the Feed, some work exclusively with Stories, others take advantage of the IGTV video platform, or really creative, driven individuals find a balance between all three.

Setting Up an Instagram Account

Getting an account together on Instagram is quite easy, provided you have the app loaded on to your smartphone. Setting up a new account takes only a few minutes.

STEP 1   First download and install Instagram onto your smartphone from the App Store of your device.

STEP 2   Launch Instagram on your phone.

Your options for establishing an Instagram account include using your Facebook credentials, as seen in Figure 5-1, or using your e-mail. Use whichever method works best for you. The steps we outline here apply to using an e-mail to register your Instagram account.

Figure 5-1: On launching Instagram, new users can either use their Facebook credentials, or a different email or phone to launch an account.

STEP 3   Tap "Register with Phone or E-mail" and on the next screen, select either a phone number or email. Enter the preferred contact method, enter in your contact number or email, and then tap the "Next" button.

STEP 4   On receiving your Confirmation Code, enter the code in the provided field and then tap the "Next" button.

STEP 5   On the next screen, add your name so people can easily search for you and then tap the "Next" button.

STEP 6   Enter a password or passphrase for your Instagram account and then tap the "Next" button.

STEP 7   On this screen, Instagram will request your birthday. Regardless of what kind of account you are setting up, enter your birthday here and then tap the "Next" button.

If you are curious as to why you're being asked for your birthday. According to the Terms of Service, you need to be of a certain age before you can legally own an account. Additionally, Instagram and Facebook base the sponsored posts on your birthdate in order to keep the advertising appropriate. Your birthdate is kept off your profile and kept private.

STEP 8   You can either go with the Username Instagram offers, or tap "Change Username" to create an original username. Once you are set with your Username, tap the "Next" button.

STEP 9   You can build your network straight away either from your Facebook network or, progressing to the next screen, from your Contacts. Once done, tap the "Next" button.

STEP 10   Tap the "Photo" icon in the center of the screen and select a photo (or take a new one) for your Profile Picture. Choose one that best represents you as an author.

STEP 11   The next two screens offer you another chance to build your network with popular accounts you may enjoy. You can either follow them or choose to skip.

You will see immediately that Instagram is not designed as a desktop app, but more for "capturing it instantly" through your smartphone. (Now the name makes sense, right?) In fact, you cannot upload photos or videos from your computer—all your Instagram posting has to be done through your smartphone.

Once you see a list of new images to look at, your account is ready to go so let's check out some of this platform's options.

Getting to Know Instagram

Take a look at the menu bar running along the bottom of Instagram. These five icons are all the options you need to get around the Instagram app, build your Instagram network, and interact with others.

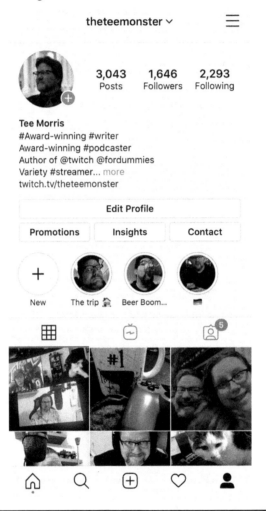

Figure 5-2: The Instagram Profile is your first impression to other Instagram users, so a complete profile is the best kind of profile to have on the platform.

From left to right, your icons are as follows:

Home—The Home icon takes you to your Timeline of Instagram users. Their posts will appear here. You will also see an inbox icon, which is where you can send and receive direct messages.

Explore—If you want to check out and follow popular accounts on Instagram, search for users you might know on Instagram, or look up hashtags people are attaching to their images, you can view hashtags in the Explore option by tapping on the Compass Rose icon.

Post—When you are ready to post a photograph with Instagram, tap the center Post icon. You will be immediately routed to the Photo mode where you can take a photograph with Instagram. Tapping on the screen will establish what you want the focus point of the photo to be. You can also tap the Flip option to the left of the camera in order to take selfies (self-portraits), and you can choose a flash mode to the right. Across the bottom of the post screen, you can switch to Video (located to the right) or access your phone's Library (located to the left).

Notifications—The speech bubble with the heart is where you go to receive and track Notifications. There are two modes here: Following and News. Keep your Notifications on News in order to see who's following you and to track who Likes your photos.

Profile—This final icon is where you can edit your profile. Once in your profile, edit your Preferences by tapping the gear icon in the top-right corner of your smartphone. This option also lets you find out what photos you've been tagged in.

The Profile, like other profiles you will find online, is the place where you can introduce yourself. As pictured in Figure 5-2, your name, a brief bio, and a relevant link are offered to people who want to know more about you before following. You can edit this content at any time from your account or from the app by tapping on the Profile icon on the far right of the menu bar and then tapping the "Edit Your Profile" option.

Before we drop in our first post, let's finish working on the Profile. We should have a complete introduction for people who find us on the platform. There is a lot we can share in our Profiles, but even here, a strategy is in play.

STEP 1   Tap on the far-right icon in the Instagram menu to access your Profile, if you are not there already. Once at your Profile, tap the "Edit Profile" button.

STEP 2   Tap your current Profile Photo to change it.

Similar to Twitter, your Profile Photo should have some thought behind it, some considerations before going with "a really cool photo" either from your Library or from Facebook:

- Use pictures taken either from the chest or neck up.
- Avoid images with busy backgrounds.
- Avoid offensive imagery.
- If you decide to use a logo, make sure your logo is original and your own.
- Avoid text-heavy or busy images as personal logos.

STEP 3   Once you find a photo that works for you, crop it accordingly and post.

STEP 4   Tap on your Name and edit your name either as the name you go by, your pen name, or a combination of both.

STEP 5   Tap on your Username and edit your username to either match other profiles on social media, or change your online ID completely.

Remember: Consistency makes finding you online that much easier. If your username on Instagram can match other profile, do so here.

STEP 6   Tap on the Website field and enter in your URL.

You can associate one URL with your account.

 While you are only allowed one URL, you can continuously change your URL to meet your needs. Say you have just posted a new blogpost? You can go on and enter in the post's link in your profile, then post something in your feed where you point people to "the link in my Profile." You can also create short links to latest releases, podcast appearances, or recent columns. The URL can go where you want to take people from week to week, if you so desire.

STEP 7   Tap on your Bio and enter in a brief bio about yourself.

Whether you are doing your bio as a small paragraph or line-by-line, you are limited to 150 characters. Hashtags, as seen in Figure 5-3, are active so you can also incorporate them.

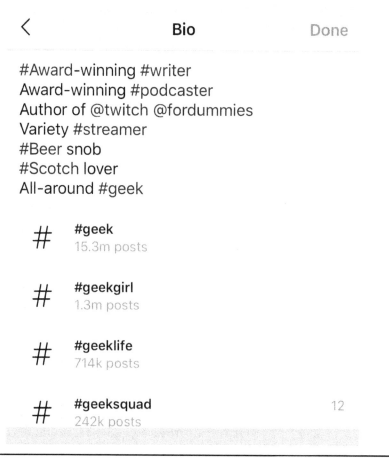

Figure 5-3: Bios are limited to 150 characters and can feature active hashtags in order to help people find you on the platform.

STEP 8   Tap the Done option, located in the upper-right corner to save any changes.

With your Profile complete, you can introduce yourself to people new to your titles, or confirm to fans of your books that this is the right account. You don't have to share all details of your life, or where you live, or what your interests are. You do want to let people know, though, that this particular Instagram is yours. So, give your Profile some thought.

Now we get to posting photos with Instagram. More importantly, let's look at how we can take a photograph with the app and then share the photo across a number of social networks.

Posting a Photo on your Instagram Feed

Whenever you take a photo with your smartphone's camera, you have a potential post with Instagram. If you have not posted anything yet, you should be in Photo mode. We're going to actually work with our Photo Library as the photos taken there give us a little more image to work with than Instagram's built-in camera.

STEP 1   Tap on the *Post* option and then tap on the *Library* option.

STEP 2   Find a photo you want to work with. Tap and hold your thumb on to the image and drag up and down. Then take your index finger and thumb and place them on the image, and spread them apart to zoom into the image. This is how you can manipulate or crop the image. When you have the image you want, tap Next.

STEP 3   *Filters* are now available across the bottom of your screen. You can review these filters by swiping left or right across the previews underneath your image. Tap the *Nashville* filter to apply it to your image.

Instagram lets you see exactly how the photo will look with the filter applied before you commit to it.

STEP 4   Double-tap the Nashville filter icon to access the filter's preferences. Tap the square located to the far-right of the slider. The Border option turns blue, and adds the stylized border to your image. The slider controls the intensity of the applied filter. Go on and adjust the slider to find a setting you like, then tap Done.

Each filter has a stylized frame. Take a look at each filter and see what you like to work with.

Figure 5-4: Filters have unique borders associated with them. They can either give your image a look as coming from a filmstrip (like *Nashville*, seen here) or even a brushed edge.

STEP 5   Tap Next to reach the *Share* window. Compose a caption for the photo in the field next to the thumbnail of your photo. At the end of your caption, add at least two hashtags related to your photo, then tap OK in the upper-right corner of the screen.

STEP 6   Tap *Name This Location* to tag your location.

STEP 7   As seen in Figure 5-5, tap each network where you want to share this image alongside Instagram.

There are four social networks you can connect to your Instagram:

- Facebook
  Twitter
  Tumblr

These three networks are covered in-depth within this book, so you should know what they are and how they fit into your social media strategy.

- Mixi

Mixi, based in Japan, offers many of the same services as Facebook, only with expanded options to keep your content private.

If you have not connected your networks to Instagram as yet, the app will walk through a login process. This connection you will only have to do once. After you sync your social media networks into Instagram, you can now share your Instagram posting across multiple networks with a single tap.

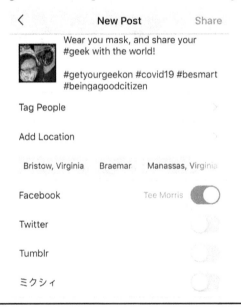

Figure 5-5: Instagram allows for cross-posting where your image and caption can appear across multiple social media platforms.

STEP 8   Tap "Share" to post your image.

 The Tag People option is best used only after your network is up and running. This is how you can tag friends who appear in the image. Notification of tagging appears under your Profile.

Here's the appeal of Instagram: taking a simple image and getting creative with it. This platform gives amateur photographers the chance to have some fun with images in their camera roll. Your posts appear instantly on an individual's Feed while simultaneously appearing on Facebook and Twitter if you decide to cross-post. Many popular mobile apps—Pinterest, YouTube, Yelp, Starbucks, Vivino, and Untappd, for example—allow for cross-posting.

You would think those two aspects alone would be enough to make Instagram your own, but there is a third aspect of the app that works for authors: *Stories*. More in the vein of Snapchat, Instagram Stories are temporary images or video clips that can either notify of upcoming events you want to promote or releases about to happen for you. Stories are quick hits that alert your network that you have just posted an update; and as Instagram is integrated with Facebook, you can also drop your Stories in Facebook as well.

Posting a Photo on Instagram Stories

The trick of Instagram Stories is the time limit—15 seconds. Without thinking ahead, you may post a story that is text-heavy (and yes, it happens often) and only get to the second paragraph before you move on to the next image. Yes, you can jump back to the image; but you don't want your audience to struggle with your Stories.

So, let's not only go into posting a Story, but getting a bit more time out of your images and video segments.

STEP 1   Go to Instagram and look at the top of your main feed. To the far left of a row of IG profiles from your network is your Profile picture with "Your Story" underneath it. Tap that icon to enter "Create Stories" mode.

You can shoot live video, take a new photo, or use photos and video from your smartphone's camera roll. For this exercise, we will be using images from our camera roll.

STEP 2   Tap the "Camera Roll" icon (a thumbnail of your most recent picture) located in the lower left of your screen. Find a photo on your Camera Roll you want to work with. Tap the photo to bring it into your Story.

Figure 5-6: When creating a Story, Instagram gives you a simple design grid to work with as well as a simple Delete tool at the bottom of your screen.

STEP 3   Tap the Text tool (the "Aa" icon) and type a simple message for your image. No more than three sentences. When you finish typing, tap the *Done* option.

When you type your message, it is white by default. When you finish typing your sentence, you can tap any of the icons located above-center and lower-right to change attributes of your text, pictured in Figure 5-7. At the top-center of the screen is the style of text you are using. Tap on these text tools and try out different looks for your text. Finally, there is a slider to the left-hand side of the screen. Tap-and-drag the slider up or down to make your text larger or smaller.

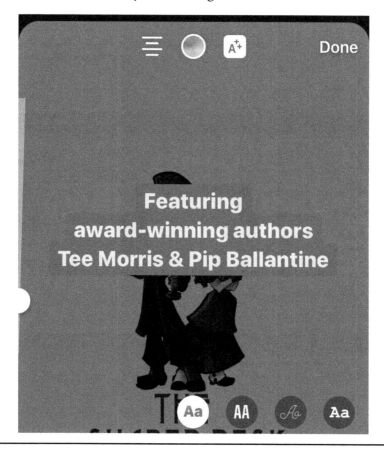

Figure 5-7: Text tools located to the top-center and bottom-right of your image features many options to help you create captions and messages.

STEP 4   Tap and drag the text to where you want it to be in your image.

STEP 5   Tap the *Send To* button; and from the list offered, tap the *Share* button next to the *Your Story* option.

STEP 6   Tap the Done button.

STEP 7   Tap on the "Your Story" icon in Instagram again, and then tap on your Profile Pic icon located in the upper left of the screen to return to "Create Story" mode.

STEP 8   Find the same image you just used, and repeat Steps 3-7 three more times. Each image should feature a different message.

STEP 9   When done, tap "Your Story" and review your story.

When you look at your Instagram Story, a one-minute story similar to the one pictured in Figure 5-8, you will notice the image appears as one continuous cut while only your titles change. With a simple message on each image, your audience has time to read your story without processing a new image. The story is clean, simple, and easy to read. Your Story also appears on Facebook.

Figure 5-8: A Story can take advantage of one image and changing text to promote an upcoming event. Each clip is 15-seconds (as depicted along the bottom of the image) but the total message is a full minute (depicted across the top).

Experiment with Instagram Stories. You can take photos or even video with the Story mode's camera. You can also create *Boomerangs*, looped video that lasts a few seconds before leading to another video or still image. From animated stickers to audience polls to a revolving library of filters, Stories ramp up your Instagram game.

Just remember that your Stories are available only for 24 hours. The next day, your Stories are a clean slate and you can create again.

Beyond Instagram: Third-Party Apps

Throughout the book and in our Do's and Don'ts chapters at the end of the manual, we recommend avoiding third-party applications that simply copy-and-paste your message into other platforms. Automation is a good thing in moderation, but it should not be the only way you work on other platforms. You want your network to know there is a real person on the other end of these updates, tweets, and posts, accessible and open for engagement.

Instagram is an exception to this rule. There are many third-party apps available either geared specifically to Instagram or for the photographs and video in your smartphone to make them "Like" Magnets for other Instagrammers.

Layout

It's one thing to post a truly break-taking picture on Instagram, but what if you are in the middle of a book event and can't take a break to post? Or what if you reach the end of a weekend convention or writers' retreat, and suddenly remember you have Instagram on your phone? Here is where you impress your network with a snappy collage of images, and *Layout* is the app that not only helps you create it, but preps your collection of images for Instagram. If Layout is not installed, tapping the grid layout icon in Instagram (located in the lower right corner of the photo preview) will take you to the app for you to install. Layout gives you a collection of frames ranging from symmetrical to creative. Once you've designed your collage, Layout connects to a variety of platforms to where you can export Instagram, Facebook, Twitter, and others.

Collages are eye-catching and fun to put together. They also tend to bring in more Likes and Comments.

Vidstitch

Layout takes your Instagram to the next level by creating sharp, slick collages. *Vidstitch* is the next step, this time adding the element of video into your collages. Vidstitch allows you to incorporate in one frame of your collage a small video clip. With an in-app purchases, you can expand your gallery of frames to include widescreen images, allowing for more still shots to accompany your video; or upgrade the Vidstitch app to the "Pro" version, allowing you to create a collage of videos. The interface and workflows for Vidstitch are a touch more complicated than Layout, but with a bit of practice you can create some eye-catching, engaging content for Instagram.

Repostly

With the ability to share postings on Facebook, retweet on Twitter, and reblogging on Tumblr, you would think Instagram would offer this function but presently it does not. That is a shame as some Instagram photos you may come across are nothing less than stunning, or others that just capture a mood that you want to share with your network. The app *Repostly* allows you to easily share images from other Instagram accounts, working as a retweet function for Instagram. In the spirit of proper accreditation, Repostly watermarks the image with its original Instagram account, and populates the Post window in your Instagram with the original accompanying post. You can edit the post, or clear it completely, but the image will have the original Instagram account from where it came from. For images that you think your audience would enjoy, Repostly is a great option for sharing the work of others and providing engaging content of your own, making it a must have in your third-party applications for Instagram.

Iconosquare

Iconosquare (https://pro.iconosquare.com) offers you a deep look into what is in your feed, who you are following, and how other Instagrammers are reacting to your content. Analytics are collected on Followers you have picked up, which Followers have dropped you, how your most recent post compares to previous ones and which images are seeing the most engagement. Iconosquare also allows users outside of the Instagram app to fully manage their account. You can "Like" photos from your feed, follow and unfollow other Instagrammers, reply to comments, and even perform a Repost function similar to the Repostly app. Iconosquare can also post your images on a variety of social media platforms, making the website and app an essential tool for success with Instagram.

Best Practices on Instagram

Instagram, while authors are posting, reposting, and commenting, is a social media outlet writers either do not seriously consider as a viable promotion platform or try it out for a brief spell, have a bit of fun, and then forget they have the app on their smartphone. With the right approach and application, though, Instagram can provide a treasure trove of visual content for a writer. Now before you think that "visual content" for a writer consists of nothing more than a picture of your laptop with your work-in-progress on the screen, cast a more imaginative net. Instagram posts can go beyond a writer's desk or book signings. Your feed can include character inspirations, behind the scenes in research or travel, and even a quick nod back to your blog. What is key is how you approach your content.

Upcoming Releases, Special Events, and Cover Reveals

Have you got a date for your next novel, or have you gotten the approval of your publisher to reveal your next book cover? Instagram can easily allow you to share artwork pertaining to your upcoming launch. Whether it is an original graphic cooked up in the image editor or a cropped section of your cover, Instagram—with Iconosquare added into the mix—gives you the ability to send out a single post across seven social networks, the post pointing back to one central location be it your blog, a link to where pre-orders are being taken, or anywhere within the Internet. You can also create original artwork publicizing special events—a Kickstarter, a charity anthology, or an upcoming appearance—where you will be participating. The image you create for Instagram can also serve as your own branded artwork for the event in question.

Author Appearances

Book signings can only be so interesting. Maybe a snapshot of you with pen at the ready and books arranged neatly, but then what? Depending on the appearance and the location, quite a bit. If you are appearing with other authors on a panel discussion, you can take quick photo of the discussion. After the panel, why not a candid shot with the other authors or editors attending? (Make sure to spell names right, and ask if they are on Instagram so you can tag them accordingly!) You can also post images documenting your travel to various conventions and conferences where you will be presenting, geotagging where each of these moments are taking place and inviting readers within driving distance to join you there. Provided you know of other writers of Instagram attending the event with you, you can repost images or video from their feed to boost the signal.

Figure 5-9: Instagram, as it works best in the moment, is a great way of promoting and documenting appearances, like Balticon where Tee and Pip frequently open up shop.

Competitions

Competitions are a proven way to increase followers on Instagram, but wait to do this after you have at least a small following; it will be hard to make a splash if you are only being followed by a few people. Right off the bat, Instagram is nice enough to lay out rules for promotional guidelines at https://help.instagram.com/179379842258600 so always keep those in mind while designing your giveaway.

User generated content competitions are popular on Instagram, and a great way to encourage creativity among your followers. They also have the advantage of not running afoul of any local laws governing sweepstake competition.

In order to fit in all the rules, prizes, and what you want entrants to do, you should create a post or page on your blog or website. You then put this URL in your Instagram post. In there will also be the hashtag that you are using to keep track of entrants.

So, what do you ask people to do? Keep it simple, and make sure it involves nothing dangerous or too outrageous. A picture of them with the book (book selfies), or dressing up like a character are some good choices. Or you could go with something related to your genre that is more open to interpretation. Take a picture of love, or joy.

Make sure the prize is enticing enough. It doesn't always have to be expensive. Advanced Reader Copies make great prizes, or a selection of items related to your book. Writer Starla Huchton (http://www.starlahuchton.com) has written books about superheroes, and often gives away well thought out prize packs of items with superhero themes.

Now go make your own graphic to post on Instagram, and make sure it is attention grabbing, and contains the hashtag you have come up with.

Don't forget to spread the word about your competition over all your other networks.

Community Building

Some authors have taken on the monumental task of creating Instagram challenges. The host author will create an original hashtag (#whyshewrites from @shewritesdotcom, for example) and posts a daily challenge for authors to create an image and accompanying post that answers the challenge. Examples of these challenges include:

- My Best Writing Day
- Elevator Pitch
- My "Go To" Relaxation
- When I'm not writing . . .

With these author challenges, you can build a following around your challenges, the hashtag you create, and your brand. This is also a great way of growing your network and building a community, but make sure this strategy is something you have time to develop. You are going to be creating unique, daily challenges for writers every month. If you're time to write is sacred and already tough to manage, confirm that you can do this on your current editorial schedule.

Author challenges are a great way to build your community and your network of authors. You also get a great look at the creativity many authors possess. It's a real exercise of expression when you visualize your inspiration or a current work-in-progress, and can introduce you to some really neat people all sharing a passion for writing.

Figure 5-10: Writers like Debra Torres create monthly Author Challenges that serve as great network and community builders.

Teasers and Motivationals

Selections from your upcoming release are always great in getting readers excited; but in the social media arena, authors need to grab a reader's attention. In the same way graphic designers pull choice quotes from a magazine article to grab a reader's attention, authors are now using juicy character quotes and small chunks (no more than three sentences) of narration to tease their readers with what is to come in their next work. Teasers work here the same way Hollywood tantalizes rabid fans with iconic imagery in a movie poster—you give your readers just a hint of what is coming.

Motivationals are similar to teasers in that they are coming from your blog. While you might ask "Isn't that a little arrogant? Offering up my writing advice as sharable quotes?" Consider the motivational you create less of a "Bask in my brilliance!" graphic and more of a "This is what I want you to take away…" graphic. On Instagram, Motivationals and Teasers are terrific promotions for your novels and short stories. In accompanying posts, links are not active on Instagram; but when posted on Facebook and Tumblr with the http:// lead-in, URLs can take readers from your cross-posting to wherever you want them to go.

 Image editors offer a variety of filters and creative touches for your teasers and motivationals, but what if you can't get to your computer? You may find it hard to believe—but there's an app for this: *ImageQuote*. With a free version that watermarks the images with the ImageQuote logo and a Pro version that keeps the image logo free and also offers many more backgrounds and options, ImageQuote takes your words and lay them out in a polished, professional manner. You can also use your own smartphone photos, adjust the image, and create original backgrounds for your teasers and motivationals. ImageQuote is easy to use, easy to master, and easy to produce for your Instagram feed.

#writersofinstagram, #authorlife, #writerslife

Photos of what you're reading, what's on your computer screen, print resources on the corner of your desk, or where you are drawing inspiration from make for interesting visual content. It's a peek behind the curtain, a delightful look at what inspires you and what words are filling the page. Depending on how much you want to share, you can also post sunrises from morning walks or your view from wherever you are taking a writer's retreat.

There's a lot that going into writing a book, so why not share some of that work on Instagram? Are you heading out to the movies? Are you hosting a cookout with other creative types? Maybe you're in the convention's hotel bar or restaurant with other authors? Little moments of life like this can be fun to share with your community.

Now with tools in reach, your social media platform needs your attention. Without developing a voice and providing your networks with content, there is no platform to develop. What happens here rests on you. There is no hard and fast rule that you have to share everything. In fact, there are no hard and fast rules in social media; but there is a need for content as content is king. Without it, there is no success online. You want to be a voice and a positive, reliable resource for what you write, your genre, your interests, and your industry. Focus on developing the strongest voice possible, and your networks will provide you and your work the strongest of support.

VI: PINTEREST

YOUR ONLINE BULLETIN BOARD

Think of all the corkboards in kitchens around the world, and all the postcards, recipes, and notes pinned onto them. Now wouldn't it be nice if you had an infinite corkboard for the Internet, where you could keep all those important, pretty, and interesting items? Wouldn't it be great if you could share your corkboard with your friends, and you could see all the fascinating things they found?

The creators of Pinterest (http://www.pinterest.com) must have thought so, too. They created Pinterest as a visual bookmarking site, where people collect and collate projects and ideas, and share them with others. Each user can have multiple boards where they post things that interest them.

When it was created in March 2010, Pinterest quickly became the hot topic among its target demographic, which is women. Everyone was talking about the inspiration that evolved from sharing items with their friends. They were getting ideas for birthday parties, delicious drinks, holiday décor, and so on. In a matter of months, Pinterest.com became a very busy, very active web domain.

Think of Pinterest as a huge online bulletin corkboard, where users pin images, websites, and videos to their "boards" for others to look at and gather inspiration. Users put together as many boards as they want, based on hobbies, vacations, fashion, books, or whatever topics interest them. It is a great way for users to keep track of items they want to return to all over the Internet. These pins act as visual bookmarks, where clicking on the image is a link that will return them to the original content or display original content from the board owner.

Out of all of the social media platforms, Pinterest's demographics are very unique, leaning heavily towards females in the thirty-five to forty-four age group—and not only that the average household income of an average Pinterest user is over $100,000. Pinners are not afraid of spending money, which is always a great demographic for markets. By 2013, Pinterest had become so popular that it was estimated one third of all women in America used the site. So, if you know your target audience is women, Pinterest is a social media platform you will need to have in your online arsenal.

That is not to say men are not on Pinterest, as well. The same study found that men are more likely to read nonfiction books. Having a Pinterest board of DIY projects related to your how-to manual could provide a terrific resource for those already reading your book, earn yourself new readers from men searching Pinterest for new ideas, and keep your book relevant in providing online addendums and new ideas.

Pinterest also sports a widely spread age demographic. However as far as global reach goes, it is most popular in the United States—something that writers should keep in mind when deciding whether to add it to their marketing strategy. If your book is not available outside of there, then Pinterest is going to be of limited use to you. However, for independent authors taking advantage of a global reach, the United States is still a vital market.

While Pinterest may be one of the smaller social networks with 320 million users worldwide in 2020, it does boast passionate "pinners" who spend a good amount of time on the site—14.2 minutes per session—sharing information with each other and discussing their latest interesting discovery.

Another vital demographic trend about pinners is that they tend to buy after seeing an item on Pinterest; 83 percent of weekly users have bought an item from Pinterest. Those are great statistics for selling books; other social media platforms would be excited to have stats that good.

In summary, Pinterest is the social media platform where well-off women of all ages seek out interesting content and are happy to purchase items of interest; this is why large brand names have flocked to Pinterest. Writers can take advantage of the site in the same way.

It's time to dive into the world of Pinterest and become part of its thriving community.

The best time to pin is when the majority of your audience has time to relax with Pinterest. Analytics vary from category to category, but generally speaking the best times are Fridays and on Saturdays.

Setting Up a Pinterest Account

You can log into Pinterest using your Facebook account, but if you don't want to do that, follow these instructions:

Figure 6-1: Pinterest can set up an account from scratch or based around your Google or Facebook account for ease of network building and login credentials.

STEP 1	Provide your name, age, and gender.
STEP 2	Provide your country and language
STEP 3	In order to discover your interests, Pinterest has you pick at least two categories to begin with, and then five more to find out more about you.
STEP 4	Pinterest will now gather pins it thinks you will be interested in based on those initial choices.
STEP 5	Confirm your e-mail address.

With your Pinterest platform established—right now, strictly on a basic level—go to your profile and select the Settings option. Here is where you can personalize your Pinterest account. You can set your privacy settings, so Google doesn't search your pins. However, as a writer who's trying to get noticed you probably don't want to do that—the more ways people can find you the better in fact. You can decide if you want Pinterest to send you e-mail notifications when someone repins one of your pins or a selection of other activities.

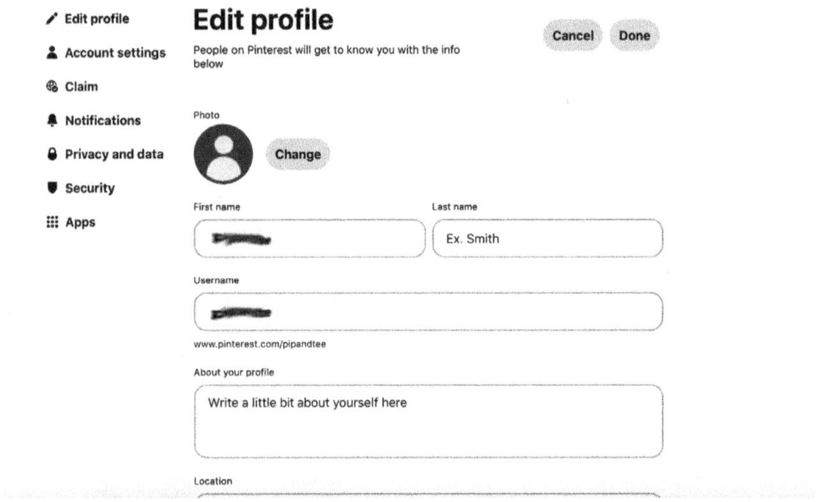

Edit profile

People on Pinterest will get to know you with the info below

Cancel   Done

- Edit profile
- Account settings
- Claim
- Notifications
- Privacy and data
- Security
- Apps

Photo

Change

First name   Last name

                        Ex. Smith

Username

www.pinterest.com/pipandtee

About your profile

Write a little bit about yourself here

Location

Figure 6-2: To make the best first impression, your Pinterest profile should be completed to the fullest. Access your profile settings in order to review, edit, and confirm your details.

Under Claim you can add your website, as well as your YouTube and Instagram.

Getting to Know Pinterest

When you first log into Pinterest, you won't see much. Only a few boards will be available, originating from your suggestions as a new pinner, but soon enough you'll be pinning from all over the place. Let's look over the layout.

Figure 6-3: Your Pinterest bar may seem somewhat basic, but you can control many aspects of this platform from here.

If you want to share a board (for instance with a publicist, co-writer, or your PA) then simply go to your board, click "Edit Board," and add the e-mail of that person under collaborators. Once they have accepted your invitation, they will be able to pin to your board, and you can set about making magic together ... or at least an interesting board.

On the right now should be your "Edit Profile" button. Use this if you want to tweak your profile in any way after the initial set up.

Next to that, the gear icon is your account settings if you want to change your original setup. If you have converted your personal account into a business one, then this is where you will access your analytics information. It's also the place to create a widget code to place into your own Web page. Finally, you can also log out here, but that's not something you have to do unless you have multiple accounts.

Back on the main page, the last icon next to your name is a double pin icon. This is where you access News (what other people are doing), You (what other people are doing with your information, repinning, liking, and also anyone you know through other networks who has just joined Pinterest), and Messages. Unlike some other media platforms, you're not likely to get too many messages, but do keep an eye on it.

Finally, and most importantly, in the bottom left of the page is a plus symbol. This is where you can upload images directly, or from the Web, and create another board. Remember, while a pin is an image or video, a board is a collection of pins. Keep that kitchen corkboard in mind and it'll be easy to remember.

Now that we've had a quick tour of the Pinterest neighborhood, let's see what we can do with it.

Working with Pinterest

Like all of the social networks, the key is community. Luckily Pinterest makes it very easy to go out and find your community.

First of all, search "authors," "writers," or "INSERT YOUR GENRE HERE books." You can choose to follow the boards you find, but if you check a little deeper into the owner of the board, you might find other common interests. You can choose to follow all, or just some, of their boards.

As we said in earlier chapters, don't just stick with your colleagues. Broaden those horizons! Find people who share other interests with you as well. The most popular pins on the site are Cooking and Dining, DIY and Crafting, Health, Funny Stories, Beauty and Fashion, and Technology.

Find some boards and pinners that you find interesting and follow away. If you do so, your pin stream will be full of interesting pictures and videos. These are great resources for repinning.

When you click on a pin, it will become much larger, and if you click again, if there is a link, you will be taken to that site.

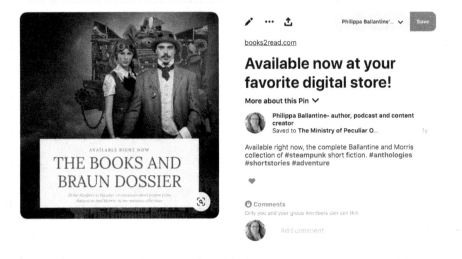

Figure 6-4: For the Books & Braun anthology, the pin created offered a link to the book.

It's a good idea to check links because some less moral pinners might try a bait-and-switch on links—or the link might have been removed or moved. Remember you want to provide your audience with great content, so it's worth it to take a moment to examine what you are repinning.

Repinning is a great way to enhance your feed and the community, and to pad how often you are marketing those books of yours.

It really is very simple. When you hover over other people's pins, you click the "Save" button. Then you have a choice of which board you want to pin to and whether you want to add a description.

Like other social media platforms, commentary is a good idea. You can put the original information in some square brackets and then put your comment before or after that. In this way, you preserve the original pinners words, which makes you a good community member. Your comments can be as simple as "I'm going to try and make these muffins!" to "This looks like a dress my heroine in INSERT MY TITLE would wear."

It is always good Pinterest etiquette to credit your sources if you can. Also, using other peoples' images but linking to your blog or Web page is an underhanded practice and can inspire people to leave negative comments. Don't do it if you want to develop a good Pinterest reputation.

You can also click the up arrow next to the link name, and from here you can send the pin directly to a Pinterest contact, or to either other social media, or via email. Use this feature with caution, and never try and spam people with your pins! Under this menu you can also just copy the URL of the link if you'd like to check it out directly.

Making Your First Board

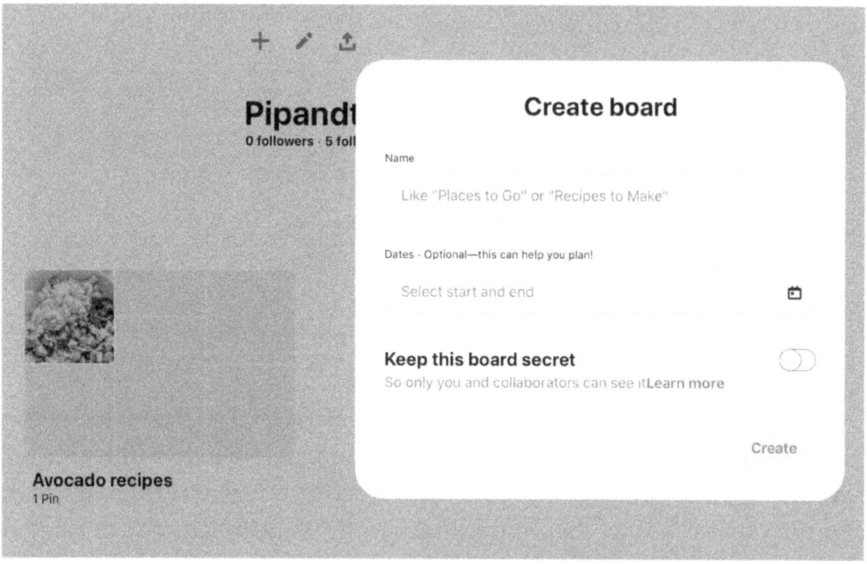

Figure 6-5: Boards can serve as organizational tools in Pinterest.

Creating Boards on Pinterest is easy, and don't be afraid of making too many. The more boards, the more interests, and the more views. From your profile, click on the large grey plus sign with "Create a board." From here give your board a name and give it an optional start date. Then decide if you want to make this a secret board rather than a public one. Secret boards are great for saving items to pin later, or for boards about projects you're not quite ready to talk about yet. You can also add in collaborators, and choose if they can add new members to this board themselves.

Uploading a Pin of Your Own

Now to the exciting stuff, let's add some content of your own. Book covers, fan art, images of people you'd like to see play your characters, places where you have set your books—all of these make excellent uploads.

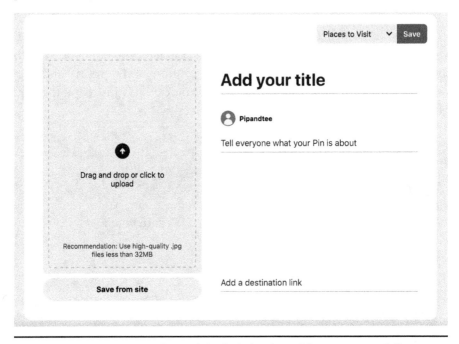

Figure 6-6: Creating your first original pin begins with an easy-to-follow template.

Click on the plus icon and choose the image by either dragging and dropping it into the grey square, locating it on your computer, or giving Pinterest the URL of the image direct from the website you found it on (which could be your page!). It can be a GIF, JPEG, or PNG file. Choose the board you want to add it to, or create a new board for this image . . . but only if it fits in with your interests. Too many boards with only a few images are not enticing.

The important part of this pin is the description. Keep in mind what your readers might be looking for. Include a substantial description about what this image means to you. Don't forget a couple of hashtags, and if it is relevant, now is the time to insert a link. The link should lead back to your website, if not link to a location where the all-important impulse buying can be made.

Finally, if you have connected other social networks, you can choose to post it there.

There—you've done it. You have your first original pins!

Tools of the Trade: Pinterest Applications

Pinterest is best described as a virtual bulletin board, an unassuming image for a website, but don't be fooled. There's a lot happening there. Once you establish your profile and get all your details online, it is best that you explore and (subsequently) master the nuts and bolts of your Pinterest account. While there are a few features and options worth mentioning, the good news is they are extremely user-friendly.

As we are deep into this book, you may see a pattern when it comes to your profiles and accounts. You want your usernames, profiles, and profile pictures to all follow the same look and feel so that when you tell people "You can find me online at..." you only have to give one screen name. If you do find yourself in need of creating new profile names for yourself, the reoccurring profile picture and simple bio will let people know they have found you. When it comes to profiles, you adhere to the two Cs: completion and consistency.

The Browser Button. There is one piece of useful equipment you should have before you begin pinning in the wilds of the Internet. The button goes in your browser and makes pinning things on the Web much easier. Go to https://about.pinterest.com/en/browser-button and click on "Get our browser button" and then "Add to (Chrome/Firefox/Microsoft Edge)." Now when you click on the Pin icon button, you will find a selection of the images that you can pin. Choose the best one, click to Pin, choose a board it fits with, then add a description.

The Widget. In order to spread the word about your pinning activity, the site offers a choice of widgets.

- Save—To allow visitors to your website to pin images easily to their boards.
- Follow—Let's people follow you on Pinterest.
- Pin widget—To embed one of your pins on your website
- Profile—Shows off up to 30 of your latest pins.
- Board—Displays one of your boards.

To find this widget, you can simply go to Pinterest at https://developers. pinterest.com/tools/widget-builder/?type=pin

The Mobile App. Pinterest has a great app for on-the-go pinning from your smartphone. The app is available for both Android and iOS. Anything you can do on the Pinterest website, you can do from the comfort of your smartphone. You get the full stream of the boards you are following, and after clicking on any of them, you can repin straight to your boards— including any secret ones (later in this chapter, we'll discuss how to use these). In addition, you get the choice of saving the picture to your phone, copying the link, or sending it to someone else on other social networks. This is useful if you are writing a blog post on the subject while you're out and about. You can also search, create a pin from scratch, receive notifications, and access all your boards by clicking on your account icon.

With these basic tools under your belt, you can accomplish a lot with Pinterest; but how? Sure, you can pin your book cover, inspirational artwork, and images from your various events, but what will bring people to you boards and keep them there? Preferably for longer than 14.2 minutes a day?

Game On: Pinterest Competitions

Pinterest has become one of the go-to sites for winning items, and they don't try and charge you for the privilege of promotion. Pinterest is happy for pinners to use their boards for marketing, however the rules have tightened in the last few years. Now Pinterest asks you to follow these rules.

- Don't suggest Pinterest is sponsoring or endorsing the competition.
- Don't require that the participants post a specific image.
- One entry per participant.
- Makes sure your participants use the words 'competition' or 'sweepstakes.'

We'd also strongly suggest you be strategic with competitions—in other words, don't run them all the time. Instead use pinning contests for marking important events, like book releases or holidays, or for making bestseller lists!

Calculate how much money you can afford to spend on a contest. The larger the prize, the more entries and reach you are likely to have. Keep in mind the interests of Pinterest users, and keep what you are asking them to do relatively simple. Nothing is more frustrating for a reader than jumping through hoops.

Before deciding what sort of contest you want to run, settle on what your goal is. Are you trying to get more people to your website? Do you want to get more subscribers to your e-mail list? Or are you just trying to increase book sales?

Ideas for Pinterest Competitions

Create a Wish List Board. Run a competition asking pinners to create a "wish list" board with your book on it, along with other books of a similar genre. Ask them to include a hashtag so you can find who has created the lists. This is especially good as it encourages friends and family of the pinner to purchase the book for them. At the end of the promotion, give away something of a decent dollar value, like a Kindle. You can choose a winner randomly, or judge the boards and pick a winner. Also keep an eye on Pinterest's terms and conditions (which are constantly being updated), just so you don't break any rules.

Books in the Wild. Build buzz for your book release by asking pinners to post pictures of the book in the wild, out in bookstores or with the reader themselves. All those pins appear in their friends' feeds, hopefully resulting in more followers and greater awareness of your book. Again, post simple rules and create a hashtag so you can find the entries.

It's Business Time: Pinterest Business

As an author, you are a business, and Pinterest Business offers layers of depth that go above and beyond individual accounts. It is probably a good idea that you become familiar with the basic site before you jump into converting to a business account, but once you do, the options are thrilling.

STEP 1   Claim your website by click on the three dots in the top left corner. Go to "Settings" and then "Claim."

STEP 2   Input your website URL in the "Claim website" section. After clicking "claim" select, "add HTML tag." Copy that tag and click "Next."

STEP 3   Now you will need to go into the inner workings of your website. Go to the index.html file and add that tag into the <head> section.

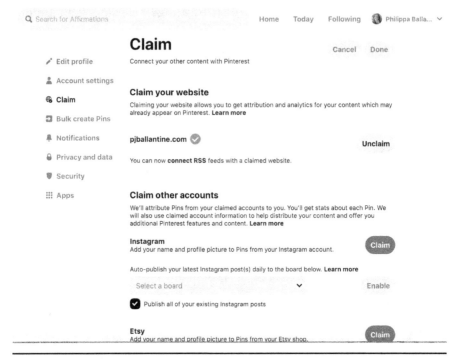

Figure 6-7: Now it's business time for your Pinterest account.

If you need help, Pinterest has a list of instructions for a variety of popular website hosts https://help.pinterest.com/en/business/article/claim-your-website#section-12106. In exchange for a little bit of work, you will get some large advantages.

Pinterest Analytics

Here you can see your daily impressions (how often your page is loaded) and viewers for a whole year. It's always nice to be able to see trends and to observe how well your strategy is working. It will also give you the top pin impressions and top boards with pin impressions from the last thirty days, so you can see what images and videos are attracting pinners. Look for trends. Try to find what it is about your popular pins that bring people to your boards. You can also access the same data on repins and clicks.

You can even break it down by the devices that people are using. Are your followers reading on a desktop, mobile or tablet? You can easily find out, and it is useful for working out which sort of pins are getting the most engagement.

Your Audience. Once you've seen information about your pins, you can find out more about those who viewed them. For instance, how engaged they are, which country they live in, as well as their sex, their language, their metro area, and even what subjects they are interested in. The online trends and behaviors of Ministry of Peculiar Occurrences pinners, for example, have indicated that they are fond of recipes, fashion, art, and DIY home decor.

Analytics will have you register a site and verify it. Once that's done, it will track how many views you are getting from blog posts pinned to your boards. Then you will be able to see which are your top blog post pins. Those pins should give you some idea of what your board followers find most interesting. Take note of those posts' images and key words, and use them in future posts to get the most views.

Other Business Tools. Pinterest Business accounts offer advantages outside of analytics as well.

Save Button. Useful if your website host doesn't have the button integrated into posts. Tumblr, Blogger, WordPress, and Wix all should, however. This button provides a quick and simple way for readers to pin your post.

Scheduled Pins. You can pre-load content and set when it goes live.

Advertising. You can pay to promote your pins.

Watching Where You Point That Pin: Pinterest Strategies

Pinterest strategies are all about making the most of the visual medium and the community. As a writer, you might think you don't have many visual resources to mine, but with a little creative thinking and the Internet at your disposal, you'll soon find it is easier than you think to fill up a board with some pin-worthy pieces.

Readers love to crawl inside the mind of their favorite—or newly discovered—writer. So, let them in!

Now Boarding: Book, Series, and Character Boards

Create a board for each of your books or series, and display your inspiration. Think of it as the bonus features to the book. Pin photos of locations that inspired the stories, costumes that you imagine the characters wearing, historical images (if your book is history based), reviews, podcasts, fan art, and book covers.

If you want to start pinning before your book comes out, make the board a secret one. When you are ready to announce the publication of your book, you will simply edit the board to be public and, voila, you have instant content for your readers! If you want to go further, you can create boards for individual characters. Fill these boards with insights into who the characters are, including books they might want to read, fashions they'd wear, or even decor they would have in their apartment.

Readers also love a sneak peek behind the curtain: Traditional publishers might not let you reveal unfinished or draft cover images, but if you are self-publishing, you get to make these decisions. Consider pinning cover image ideas, drafts, a list of movie stars you'd hire to play the characters in a movie of your novel. You can even ask readers to comment on what they think.

As with any social media, you should make your boards attractive and reflective of yourself. Have one for characters, one for settings, and one for series, but also make boards dedicated to your other interests: fashion, cooking, travel, or something connected with your writing, like costuming or history. Different boards are a great way to show how diverse a person you are—don't be afraid to let your personality shine through.

In conjunction with making it look good, always ensure you only pin quality material. Readers will know that you care about your content and will return for more. Make sure you use your Pinterest account for more than mere marketing. You'll also need content that you find on other boards. Content curating (dealt with later in this book) is the latest strong trend, and it can help make your boards a go-to location for your readers.

From Literal to Figurative: Mood Boards

Other popular boards—like mood or color boards—can also be used to market your book. It is surprising how many pinners are looking for boards that have themes on feelings, rather than subjects. It is something a little out of the ordinary, appealing to different senses. For example, you might make a mood board for your horror novel and call it "Creepy." Then you'd fill it with things that frighten you. If your book is a romance novel, you might make a board called "Joy" and populate it with fun and beautiful images. Color boards are popular with designers, but they will only work for you if you create something that fits in with your book. If your words were colors, what would they be? These boards will attract DIY and fashion enthusiasts, and those people read, too.

In the case of mood or color boards, don't forget a good, strong description, with that all-important website URL in it. People looking for inspiration might be curious enough to follow it.

Secret Pins: Keep It Secret... Keep It Safe...

When you pin, make sure it isn't a dump of content all at once. Don't simply log on once a week, and pin fifty posts in one go. If you don't want to change to a business plan, there is a way you can avoid overwhelming your followers, and spread your pinning activities over the course of the week.

When you drop into Pinterest, you can gather all the pins you want to use, or even create your own, and pin them to this secret board. Then, later on in the week, simply go to your secret board, click on the pin, and then click on the pencil icon. Now you can move the pin from your secret board to your public ones. The pin will now appear only on the public boards.

Also, if you have a book coming out, that you don't want to quite reveal to your readers yet, this is a good way to compile some great pins for your launch day.

Tell Me About It: The Importance of Descriptions

No matter how pretty your image is, if your audience admires it and keeps going, you haven't sold a book. Make sure you offer a strong description to go with the relevant, original content you post. You can use snippets from your book, character sketches, or behind-the-scenes glimpses. Long descriptions are more engaging, and Pinterest allows you five hundred characters. So, make the most of them, and don't forget to include a link in that description!

Directing Traffic: Blogging for Pinning.

Pinterest is a great place to do cover reveals, contests, and promotions. So, don't forget to pin your blog post about these—just make sure there is an image for Pinterest to find.

If you are really stuck for ideas on what to post, a great tool is the *ImageQuote* app (covered in Chapter 5). You can take a pull quote from your post and quickly turn it into an image. It may seem a little strange to quote yourself at first, but it is an eye-catching option, especially on Pinterest.

So, from now on, make sure each blog post you write contains an image. Practice good Pinterest etiquette, even when not on Pinterest.

Images and infographics that make the best impression are vertical, tall, and use bold colors. When users are scanning down, the longer your image stays in their stream, the more likely they are to click on it.

Group Boards

Here's a good one if you want to share information with a publicist, co-writer, or perhaps a personal assistant. Boards can be shared! When creating or editing, simply go to your board, click "Edit," and add the name or e-mail of that person in the collaborators field. Once they have accepted your invitation, they will be able to pin to your board. You might want to form a shared board with your local writers' groups or authors who are in the same genre as you. It's a fabulous way to build a sense of community.

Linking Pinterest to other social media

Over the years more and more social media has become intertwined. Instagram and Pinterest has a natural partnership, with their emphasis on the visual medium. Now you can cut down some workload by linking them.

Go to the three horizontal dots in the top left corner. Click "Edit Settings" and then "Claim." From here you can link up your Pinterest (and YouTube and Etsy if so inclined.) If you have claimed your Pinterest as a business account, then the nice thing is you tick the box, to publish all of your existing Instagram posts to a board. Pip has one set up called "Writer's Life" which is a catch all for posts about writing events, covers, and a few cats and baking shots as well.

Pinterest combines visual delight with information in a way that few other social networks do. It can be a great benefit for you as a writer and a marketer. So, go get pinning, but fair warning: Once you get started, it can be quite addictive.

VII: PODCASTING

CREATING ON-DEMAND MEDIA PROGRAMS

With the many blogging sites, authors are able to get their words and inspirations out to readers. Instead of sharing those thoughts with written words, though, some authors have taken a direction by sitting down and enjoying a fireside chat with readers. That, in a nutshell, is what you're doing when you are podcasting. Podcasters create their own audio or video and syndicate it to listeners and viewers around the world, using WordPress or some other blog platform. In doing so, they become an independent production company, offering on-demand media content to subscribers via the Internet. These files are consumed by subscribers through a host website, a computer's media player of choice, or a preferred mobile device.

This is all well and good, however, many authors are not exactly dynamic in front of a microphone. Why would writers want to get into a media production platform when getting them to agree to public appearances of any kind is akin to moving mountains?

Perhaps the most obvious reason a writer would want to host her own podcast: Because he or she has something to say.

Just because the FCC doesn't have jurisdiction over podcasts doesn't mean you're exempt from the law or immune to lawsuits. You're personally responsible for anything you say, do, or condone on your show. Additionally, the rules concerning airplay of licensed music, the distribution of copyrighted material, and the legalities of recording telephone conversations all apply. You still have control over the content you create, sure, but make sure you obey the law.

Recording a Podcast with Audacity

We're keeping these steps simple in how to record, edit, and upload a podcast episode. You're going to need a computer set up with a working microphone, of course, and once that is up and running, it's time to record. We're going to use a piece of software called *Audacity* (https://audacityteam. org), a reliable open source audio recorder that offers you a lot of capabilities. Audacity is available on a variety of operating systems and it is free. After you have downloaded and installed this recorder on to your computer, take a deep breath because here's where the adventure begins.

STEP 1   Jot down a few notes on what you want to talk about.

You can make this a rough outline that includes remarks about who you are and what you want to talk about. Bullet points to keep yourself on track.

STEP 2   Launch Audacity. Check Audacity's Preferences in order to make sure your microphone is detected.

STEP 3   As seen in Figure 7-1, click the red "Record" button and begin your first recording.

Whether it is a rough text recording or an official "first episode" of whatever you are recording, go on and record with confidence.

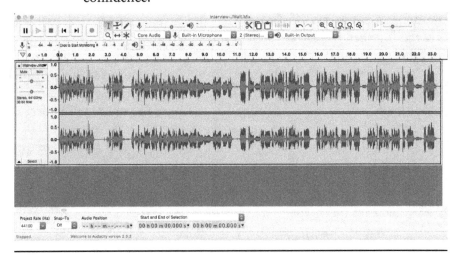

Figure 7-1: *Audacity* (https://audacityteam.org) is open source software offering a terrific, low-cost introduction to audio editing on your computer.

STEP 4   Record a sign-off like "Take care of yourselves! See you next time." and click the "Stop" button.

STEP 5   Choose "File > Save As" and give your audio project a name.

There it is—your first recording. Will it be perfect or smooth sailing? Probably not, but you will want to be patient with yourself. You may make a mistake here, or trip up on a word there. The point is you will not have necessarily a dead solid perfect recording. You may need to edit.

 When you do make a mistake in your audio — and trust me, it will happen—you should mark in your audio where this happens. This way, if you mark it in your audio, it is easy to see where it happens in your recording's waveform (the graphic representation of audio). You can either snap your fingers or click your tongue, but a handy tool for this is a pet trainer's clicker, easy to find at any pet store or online at Amazon. Use that clicker when you need to mark something in your audio.

With your less-than-perfect audio before you, let's clean up those rough points with Audacity. You will find that this software makes editing audio almost like editing text in a word processor.

Editing with Audacity

Now that you've finished recording something awesome with Audacity, you're ready to make a basic edit. Once we get this first edit done, it's a "wash-and-repeat" approach as you find another part of your audio that needs work and simply repeat these steps.

STEP 1   Find the segment that you want to edit.

 To view the entire timeline of your project, click the Fit Project in the Window tool, shown here.

STEP 2   Click the Selection tool (pictured in the margin), and then click and drag across the unwanted segment. Use the "Zoom" tool to zoom into the selection, if you need to do so.

The unwanted segment is highlighted, as shown in Figure 7-2.

Figure 7-2: With the Selection tool, click and drag across the unwanted content in the timeline.

STEP 3   Single-click the segment between your two cuts and then press the Delete key (Mac) or the Backspace key (Windows).

You can also choose Command + X (Mac) or Ctrl + X (Windows) to remove the unwanted segment.

STEP 4   Review the clip.

STEP 5   If the edit doesn't sound natural to you, undo the changes by choosing Edit > Undo or pressing Command + Z (Mac) or Ctrl + Z (Windows), and try again.

You're allowed multiple undos in Audacity, giving you the advantage to go back to the beginning point of your editing just in case you aren't happy with the sound of the edit.

STEP 6   Repeat this exercise for all of the edits you need to make throughout your audio file.

STEP 7   After your fifth edit, select File > Save or press Command + S (Mac) or Ctrl + S (Windows) to save your work.

STEP 8   When you have finished editing your project, select File > Export > Export Audio... to export your file either as an AIF (native to Mac) or a WAV (native to Windows) file.

The editing process is the most time-consuming part of podcasting, and will vary from project to project, which we discuss later on in this chapter. When you finish the final edit, you will want to review the audio. In fact, throughout the file, you will want to review. Editing audio is no different than editing a manuscript. You will want to listen to your file again and again to make sure everything sounds right. When you are done, we now need to prep the audio for uploading and delivery.

Compressing Your Audio Files

Portable media devices and computers can play *MP3 files* as a default format. While there are many other audio formats in existence, MP3 is the preferred format for podcasting. An option for preparing your final file (WAV and AIF are the most common audio formats) for podcasting is *Apple iTunes,* shown in Figure 7-3. It does many things for the podcaster, including converting a wide variety of audio file formats to MP3. Yes, it's from Apple, but the app is available for Windows users as well.

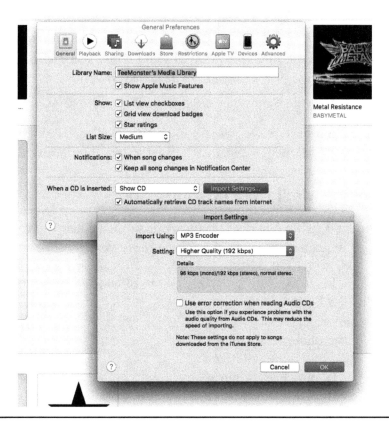

Figure 7-3: Under your Preferences Tab in iTunes, you can select what degree of compression you desire for your mp3 files.

After launching iTunes, follow these steps to convert your audio file:

STEP 1   Before working with your audio file, go to your iTunes Preferences (File > Preferences on a Mac, or Edit > Preferences in Windows) and under the General tab, select Import Settings. Change the Import Using option to MP3 Encoder.

The Settings should be at least Good Quality (128 kbps); but if you include a lot of audio design in your podcast, select Higher Quality (192 kbps). Now your files will be imported and converted to MP3.

STEP 2   Choose File > Add File to Library.

Or you can press Command + O (Mac) or Ctrl + O (Windows).

STEP 3   Browse for the audio file you want to convert and then click Open.

Your file is now in the iTunes Library.

STEP 4   Find the audio file in the iTunes Library and click to select it.
STEP 5   Choose File > Convert > Create MP3 Version.

Your file is now converted to the MP3 format.

We're almost there. We have the media prepped and ready to go, but we need to get the media uploaded in order to distribute your media.

Uploading Media and Posting a Show

After you set up a folder for your podcast media files and decide on a file naming convention, you're ready to move your freshly named files to the Web server. To do this, you need a *File Transfer Protocol (FTP)* application like *Cyberduck* or *FileZilla*, both of which support drag-and-drop file transfers.

For Cyberduck, follow these steps:

STEP 1   Choose File > Upload.
STEP 2   Browse your system to find the podcast media file you want to upload.
STEP 3   Click the Upload button.

For FileZilla, here's what you do:

STEP 1   Navigate to the desired folder using the Local Site window on the left.

STEP 2   Select one or more files and/or folders from the window directly below.

STEP 3   Drag the selected files to the Remote Site window on the left.

Simple, right? Now with your media in place, you need to post your show notes and make sure WordPress sees the file. From there, RSS does all the heavy lifting and distributes your content. We need to first get our blog set up for podcasting, and for that we need a plug-in. The plug-ins expand the capabilities of your blog, and bring a lot to what you can accomplish. For this exercise, we need a plug-in for podcasting.

So, let's get to it.

STEP 1   Return to WordPress. From your Dashboard, single-click the "Tools" option. From the expanded menu, single-click the "Plugins" option.

STEP 2   Single-click the "Search" (magnifying glass) icon. In the "Search Plugins" field, type "podcast" as your Search parameter, seen in Figure 7-4.

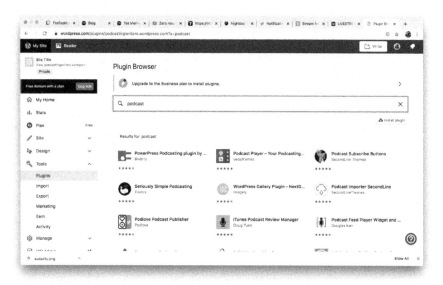

Figure 7-4: When you want to expand on the capabilities of your WordPress, plugins are a solution for what you need to get things done.

STEP 3   Select a plugin that you want to work with.

Single-clicking the plugin will give you an introduction and brief description of what it does. Find the plugin that you think will do what you need and download it for your blog.

 To install plugins, you will need to upgrade your WordPress plan. Webhosts like Dreamhost (https://dreamhost.com) have one-click plugins that make for easy integration, the cost covered in the monthly server plan.

STEP 4   Create a blogpost that covers your show notes.

Show notes are a summary of your podcast. Show notes can be a simple bullet list, a single paragraph summing up the episode, or a detailed and time coded breakdown of what is in your podcast.

STEP 5   Go to your plugin and enter in the URL of your media.

STEP 6   After a review of your episode and show notes, single-click the "Publish" option.

And there it is—your first-ever podcast episode. From here, you can take your show (and its RSS feed) to various places like Apple Podcasts, Spotify, Stitcher, and Google Play. Get your feed to the people, have people subscribe, and share your content with the world.

This tends to be the second big question we get outside of how do you podcast: What do you podcast? It's great to be able to podcast, to create new and exciting content that is all your own. However, content for content's sake is not necessarily the most compelling content. Consumers can usually pick up when the passion and the drive isn't there. So exactly what should you think about podcasting?

Writers Gone Wild: Talk Shows

A podcast talk show starts with an idea, something that the creator has the desire and knowledge to fuel with his or her own voice. Add to that a bit of passion and a do-it-yourself approach to audio or video production, and the end result is a platform for whatever the author wants to say to listeners.

And writers can produce some wickedly fun content when the right people are in the room.

Podcast talk shows are like those you might find on television or radio. They are informal, off the cuff, and sometimes even involve guests. The topics of conversation do not always have to be about the craft. Many writing podcasts start off that way, but shows we have produced in the past and appeared on as guests have covered the following:

- Book Marketing
- World Building
- Working in the Genre
- Character Development
- A Writer's Lifestyle

Writing podcasts are a bit like sitting around with your favorite authors, enjoying a cup of tea or coffee (or, if the discussion gets really informal, a glass of wine or a beer) while they talk about whatever is on their minds or while they answer questions on a certain topic. Talk shows can be very easy to produce, sometimes all that is required is a recording device and a topic of discussion.

There are two advantages to creating a simple talk show podcast:

Minimal Editing. It's just you and your guests, or just you on the mic, following a predetermined topic. You might have to edit the occasional stumble or tangent where the participants go off topic, but generally the talk show format is one of the most easy to produce. Without the need for heavy editing, it shouldn't take up much time to clean up and produce an episode. You will want to review the recording for quality and flow, of course, but sometimes you can record, edit, review, and post all in one night.

Minimal Production. Along with editing, quality concerns such as background noise (which can add to the spontaneity of the show, especially if you have cats…) are taken lightly. The talk show is more about a slice of life or a casual sit-down with literary professionals. Your main priority should be that everyone is heard clearly. Pre-planning for production can be a bullet list of talking points while your post-production should be creating show notes during the review process. Show notes accompanying the episode's blog post give listeners an idea what happens during the show. It also helps if they want to skip ahead to a specific portion or find websites you might have mentioned. Links back to these sites are always appreciated by the website's hosts.

Figure 7-5: Pip and Tee host *The Shared Desk*, a talk show about collaboration, the writing profession, and a lifestyle unique to a creative personality. (Show Art designed by Candy Cane Studios)

The biggest benefit of the talk show format, like our podcast *The Shared Desk* as pictured in Figure 7-5, is allowing your readers to get to know you, see how your creative mind works, and enjoy a sit-down with you and your guests. Making that personal connection can go a long way in social media.

Talk show formats, be they solo or panel style, are the low-production end of podcasting, but what if you decide a little polish and flair is for you. A little bit of editing, a little bit of post-production, and a lot of takes in order to get just the right reading, and you can offer something special for both fans of your work and you as a creative individual.

Anthologies in Audio: Short Stories

Thanks to podcasting, short stories enjoyed a renaissance in audio. Shows like *Escape Pod, Welcome to Night Vale, Lore,* and *The Melting Potcast* all feature short stories as part of their programming. Short fiction podcasts can be demanding, but are a great way to introduce yourself, your work, and your world to a whole new audience. As for ourselves, we produced the Parsec-winning podcast *Tales from the Archives,* a seasonal anthology set in the steampunk world of *The Ministry of Peculiar Occurrences.* We scaled down our production time by approaching the podcast with this strategy:

Stories read by the author. Each season of Tales from the Archives offers ten to twelve stories, only two written by us. The remaining short stories are written and read by authors we invite to write in our universe. To do this, we offer guidelines, editorial passes on the manuscript, and post-production services on their audio. The lion's share of the work is in the writing, recording, and editing of the short story, all of which falls back to the guest author.

Post-production Process. Once we receive an author's short story, we review the audio and then score the stories with a soundtrack and, if time allows, a few sound effects for key moments. These added production elements bring an added dimension to the stories and are choices we make as content producers in an effort to do something different, something inspired.

It is totally up to you whether you want to do a straight read or go with sound effects and music. Any elements you add into your podcasting anthology—sound effects, music, guest voices—lengthens production time. At the very least, if you are working with audio from other authors, you will want to teach yourself audio filters needed to sweeten guest audio's clarity and quality.

Biweekly Posting Schedule. As it is with blogging, a monthly schedule for podcasting tends not to be frequent enough to keep listeners engaged, while a weekly schedule consumes free time like a child rummaging through their Halloween score. A biweekly schedule, however, serves as a comfortable compromise, allowing time to produce and edit another episode while also developing new material and keeping with present editorial commitments. For all podcasts, a biweekly schedule is the easiest to keep and maintain.

Anthology podcasts work a variety of fronts, offering additional content for the book or the world that you are building. Short story podcasts take your audience deeper into the backgrounds of your characters, the subtle nuances of the world they exist in, and—in later installments of a series —reveal additional details and crossover adventures that fans relish. Bring in guest authors to write in your world and your podcast showcases more than just your work and your world, but also the creative talents of people you respect and admire.

There is one more avenue for authors to explore with podcasting, but it can be a long road ahead of you. The question is, are you ready for the journey?

Going All In: Podcast Novels

In January 2005, Tee came up with a premise that—at the time— podcasters regarded as incredibly ambitious: podcasting a novel from cover to cover. With *The Dragon Page* podcast hosting, Tee's trailblazing was joined later by young adult author Mark Jeffrey and science fiction and horror novelist Scott Sigler. In the decade that followed, writers like Mur Lafferty, P.G. Holyfield, P.C. Haring, Starla Huchton, and others undertook this challenge. When it comes to podcasting fiction, the novel remains the Mount Everest of audio projects to undertake with some authors never reaching the summit. Be it time, effort, or resources needed, final chapters remain unrecorded. For those who have completed the epic quest to recording "The End" once and for all, many takes before finally getting that perfect reading, recording when all is quiet in the house or apartment, and hours on hours of editing lie in their wake. Podcasting a novel is daunting. It is exhausting. And yes, it is exhilarating. Podcasting novels, however, is not a casual undertaking by any means.

Together, Tee and Pip produced six podcast novels—or *podiobooks*, a term coined by Evo Terra in 2005. The podiobook is exactly as you would imagine it: a novel released one chapter at a time, one podcast at a time. Some of the books we podcast were previously published while others were released as audio before they saw print. In the process of podcasting novels, we learned a few valuable lessons:

Do not launch the podcast novel until it is complete. In the early days, it was suggested that a buffer of episodes—perhaps five to ten—were good to have on hand. That way, if life happened to get in the way (and it usually would), you would still be able to keep a weekly or a biweekly delivery schedule. Now, it commonly is recommended that before the first episode launches, the podcast should be completed in its entirety. Long-form podcasting is especially difficult when attempting to maintain a regular schedule while balancing real life, so consider having your novel recorded from beginning to end before going live.

Keep production at a minimum. While indulging in various aspects of production—sound effects, guest voices, and music—is fun in short-form podcasting, long-form podcasting offers demands of its own. Such production elements will slow your progress and make completion that much harder. Keep the production in your podcast novel simple. If you want to add more elements, do so, but remember that you are increasing your workload if you do so.

With a complete podiobook, adhere to your posting schedule. With the recording and editing done, you can set your posting schedule: weekly, biweekly, twice a week, etc. In doing so, you are making a commitment to a schedule and have no legitimate reason to shirk off responsibility. Stay with that schedule.

Be careful what you wish for, or, in the case of podcasting, be careful when you ask for feedback. You're most likely to get it—and from places you may not expect. Since geography doesn't limit the distance your podcast can travel, unlike terrestrial radio, you may receive feedback from listeners coast to coast and around the world. And just like book reviews, feedback isn't guaranteed praise. Listeners will be honest with you. Respect that.

Final Thoughts on Why to Podcast

If it sounds like there is a lot of work involved in just planning and producing a podcast, it's because there is. There's no other way to put it. When an idea for a podcast comes to you, it is just like when an idea comes to you for a book. A lot of planning, effort, and resources go into a podcast; and when authors try to cut corners and run on the fly without a plan, the results can be disastrous.

Don't believe us? Search your favorite directory for the variety of podcasts about writing. You might notice some that *podfade* (a term for when a podcast starts strong, only to peter out) after a mere three episodes. When a writer's podcast includes ten minutes of a writer typing, signing books at a bookstore (without any context such as where he is, when it happened, what book he was signing, etc.), or revealing the contents of a shoe closet, you can safely assume some planning was sorely needed but didn't occur.

Yes. *A shoe closet.* We've seen a lot of bad podcasts in our day.

Podcasts can be far more work intensive than blogging, but there are definite advantages to hosting either a show or an anthology.

Podcasting fiction is a great way to introduce yourself and your work to audiences. Whether you decide to share an anthology of your backlogged short stories or your novel in its entirety, podcasts offer a "try before you buy" for potential fans all around the world. An anthology also doubles as great promotion for upcoming works, particularly a series, as the stories take nothing away from the novel you have coming; instead, these short stories introduce listeners to the world and offer glimpses at the novel's principal players. For a podiobook novel, your podcast could be a prequel or separate story running in time with the events of your main novel, offering listeners a low-risk, free introduction to your world, style, and work.

Podcasts offer audiences an intimate behind-the-scenes look at being a writer. Many still believe the author's life to be all about ascots, smoking jackets, and snifters of cognac while the sun sets. If this is true, we have failed as professional authors…

Well, we do own ascots as we write steampunk so, yeah, that's covered.

Podcast talk shows not only dispel those lofty myths, they tear down the fourth wall between writer and reader, inviting the audience into the process. Sometimes authors express themselves with breakdowns of world building, character development, and plotting. Other times, the focus is not on work but on play: what they are currently reading, a live report from a convention or author event, or two authors talking about how they unwind. The podcast is your chance to sit down with your readers and allow them to get to know you beyond your pages.

Podcasting, whether it is fiction or a variety show, is just plain fun. *"All work and no play makes Jack* (Torrance) *a dull boy,"* so why not fire up the microphones and let loose? Some of the best podcasts we have recorded have been in the studio with other authors either talking about what we do when planning and plotting, or what we do when we are off the clock. Podcasts can be very therapeutic that way, helping you manage stress, deadlines, writer's block, and a variety of other speed bumps that life can unexpectedly throw your way. You can also find joy in taking someone's audio fiction and enhancing it with music and sounds to bring it to life. And then there is the accomplishment of finishing your own podiobook, releasing it to the public, and hearing someone say, *"I heard the podcast, so I really needed to read the book."* Podcasting is a rewarding experience and, with the right plan and the right strategy, can be as equally satisfying as the release date of your latest novel.

We love podcasting and still podcast to this day. When you podcast short fiction—original episodes set within the world of your novel—these audio adventures can broaden the universe you're creating and enhance the reader's experience, provided you set a strategy. With the first season of our *Tales from the Archives* podcast, the show graphic seen in Figure 7-6, we introduced potential readers to our cog-and-gear-enhanced world through lost cases of the *Ministry of Peculiar Occurrences*. These adventures predated events of our premier novel, *Phoenix Rising*. Initially we planned for the podcast to be a glimpse into what we had created. However, when readers began asking if our audio anthology would reveal more of Wellington Books' past, the Ministry embarking on adventures in other parts of Her Majesty's empire, and whether or not there were other agencies similar to the Ministry investigating the unknown in other places in the world, we needed to change our strategy.

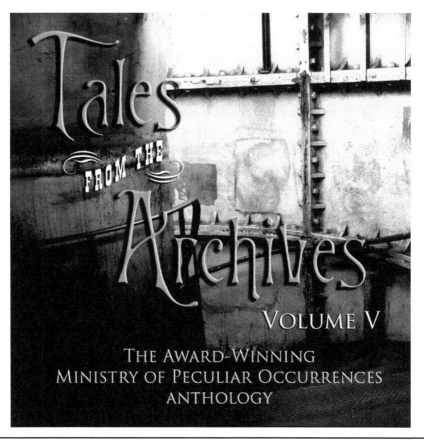

Figure 7-6: Pip and Tee's *Tales from the Archives* podcast, a steampunk anthology set in the *Ministry of Peculiar Occurrences* universe, expanded their series beyond the pages of its six primary novels.

Three of the stories from that first season—"The Evil That Befell Samson" by Pip Ballantine, "The Seven" by P.C. Haring, and "From Paris, With Regret" by Starla Huchton—went one step further and referenced events mentioned in *Phoenix Rising*. This, we discovered, was a real treat for readers as they felt the podcast offered an added dimension to the novel. Now, several Parsec Awards (an award bestowed to the best in speculative fiction podcasting), five seasons, and a "change of strategy" later, select characters, situations, and even artifacts from the podcast are making appearances in the novels, and vice versa. Some stories even carry an impact on future novels. These references (commonly known as Easter eggs) from the podcast expand a book's reach, granting you and your readers plenty of new avenues to explore. What was once a marketing tool, the *Tales from the Archives* podcast now provides a "Director's Cut" approach to the series, offering additional scenes audiences delight in experiencing.

As for our earlier-mentioned talk show, *The Shared Desk*, we employ a different strategy. There is a secondary goal of promotion—letting people know where we will be, what our upcoming projects are, and writing topics that interest us—but in the end, the aim of *The Shared Desk* is to unwind a bit. We do, and we manage events of interest to the writer while doing so. We now have the podcast down to a system that allows us to record with little-to-no post-production (although we do sometimes come across a few things that should remain unsaid and therefore must be edited out), so all that we need to do is have a topic and a chunk of time.

Author, photographer, and artist J.R. Blackwell describes *The Shared Desk* as *"just like having a drink with Tee & Pip ... "* and we take a lot of pride in that. We enjoy this connection with our readers, fans, and friends, but with deadlines, demands of family, and (of course) writing, there are occasional "silent spells" that one of our more passionate listeners, Gail Carriger, has chastised Tee for.

And when you upset Gail Carriger, you can rest assured when having tea—*no scones for you, mate.*

Podcasts can be all about promotion, but they should also be fun. With the amount of effort and planning that go into them, they should always be fun. This is the drive that keeps us going.

VIII: STREAMING

AND WE ARE LIVE!

Perhaps you are looking at the previous chapter on podcasting, you see the potential in the platform, and go all in. After some time creating episodes and sharing content, you find you're enjoying the production of a podcast. In fact, you find that you're enjoying it a lot. And after getting a season of shows out to the public, you could be wondering *"What's next?"* as there is, inevitably, something new you can explore that could help increase your reach as a writer.

After podcasting, yes, there is another platform you should consider; and what is great about this platform is that it works seamlessly within a podcast's workflow. With an adjustment to how you record and how you produce your content, your next step into producing additional content outside of your next short story or novel could very well be into *streaming*.

Streaming content usually involves working with video, but a stream can be audio only if you want a stream less demanding for playback on older computers, or mobile devices limited to slower internet connections. A less technical definition of streaming would be a platform offering consumption or broadcasting of content, either time-shifted or in real time, on a global platform. Streaming emerged shortly after podcasting, but many of the early adopters struggled to offer viewers a strong, smooth signal. With the development of broadband and technology able to handle robust data streams, streaming services now offer both audiences and content creators broadcast-quality entertainment online. There are many platforms out there to choose from, but the Big Four of streaming include:

Twitch (https://twitch.tv)—When you talk about trailblazers in streaming, Twitch is the name you hear most often. Originally a platform for video games (and still, primarily), Twitch now hosts podcasts, talk shows, and creatives of all types. The draw (and, with the right crowd, the fun) of Twitch is in the interactions your audiences can have with you, the host. Those interactions include live chat, donations and tips, and special graphic expressions with emotes.

Periscope (https://periscope.tv)—The first mobile streaming platform to appear, Periscope launched in March 2015 fully integrated with Twitter. When you go live on the app, you can send out a quick notification to everyone in your network that you are live and streaming. A few years later, Twitter's mobile app offered a live feature that notifies your network that you are streaming.

Facebook Live / Facebook Gaming (https://facebook.com)—The success of Twitch and Periscope laid the groundwork for Facebook launching in August 2015 Facebook Live, a streaming platform fully integrated with the largest social media platform in the world. Like Periscope, Facebook Live will notify your network when you go live, even offering a tiny inset video in the lower corner of your app or browser window, taking you to the stream with a single click. Facebook Gaming, a variation on Facebook Live, grants viewers the ability to interact with gamers similar to Twitch.

YouTube (https://youtube.com)—Powered by Google, YouTube was the original hub for creative video works. At one time, writers would work with YouTube when hyping their latest title with book trailers, a preview similar to movie trailers only based around your next book. With the ability to stream either directly from your smartphone or mobile device, or from a studio in your home or office, you can now stream original content (including a recording of your podcast) directly through YouTube.

There are a lot of reasons you might want to launch a streaming channel, but the simplest reason to stream, is that it's just plain fun! Tee began his own Twitch channel on September 6, 2017, and through all the breaks, the changes, and the modest numbers he's seen, he still relishes the moment he goes live, as seen in Figure 8-1. Now with Pip in the mix, the two are now creating content beyond gaming. Their own streams have included editing sessions, life advice, podcast recordings, and even the odd cooking stream. Yes, Twitch is a lot of fun.

But why would you want to put yourself up for scrutiny from a live global audience? Authors are notorious for avoiding the public eye, and many prefer the solitary lifestyle often associated with writing. Why writers should consider streaming may come as a surprise, and can make a difference in your community, both online and in the real world.

Figure 8-1: Tee takes his love of video games, writing, cooking, and podcasting to *Twitch* (https://twitch.tv) on his own channel at https://twitch.tv/theteemonster

You want to offer your audience a look behind the scenes. Streaming offers a lot of draws to people, but the creative process is becoming more and more a popular category on streaming platforms. Artists, musicians, and writers alike are going live with their works-in-progress. They are not necessarily "creating by committee" but inviting their audiences into the process, giving their approaches and reasoning behind the decisions made in creating something from nothing. For writers, it can be the building of a scene from scratch, or it can be a look at the editorial process, working with notes from an editor and explaining why some notes are worth the changes and others can be contested. When you invite your readers into the work-in-progress, you offer them a peek inside your mind and how you do what you do which makes for compelling content for your community.

Streaming seamlessly fits into a podcasting workflow. We just finished talking about podcasting, and streaming fits right into the recording process. When you hit the "Record" button on your recording software, you can go live with your stream and add in the live audience element into your podcast. The end of your stream can be the "unplugged, unedited" version of your podcast and a nice addition to your show notes, and if something goes wrong with your recording software (because no recording software application is perfect), your stream can be downloaded and the audio extracted as a backup recording. Streaming easily integrates with podcasting, and is great, lively content to offer your audience.

You want to invite your readers to an aspect of your life, off the clock. Okay, this may sound a little odd at first. You do not necessarily need to share all aspects of your life with your readers, but let's say you want to share something of interest you that has nothing to do with your writing? It could be knitting, it could be art, or it could be—as it is with Tee—a love for video games. Whatever you decide to stream, this is you outside of your "Writer" role. Maybe not entirely as Tee gets asked a few questions about writing and publishing while he's on a mission for the Vanguard, trying to stay alive in Rapture, or steering clear of Clickers and Shamblers in Seattle; but this kind of stream is a different side of you. It's that side of you you're okay with sharing, so have some fun with your fanbase and show them a talent detached from your writing.

Streaming platforms offer you a lot of options, each platform all varying in size and features, but for the purposes of *Social Media for Writers,* we focus on Twitch as this is where we create content for gamers, writers, readers, and consumers of all backgrounds coast-to-coast and around the world. The exercises featured in this book, while centric to the Twitch platform, should easily adapt to other platforms.

Creating a Twitch Account

There are two schools of thought when it comes to creating a streaming channel: The "I need the latest and greatest studio gear, the fastest supercomputer on the market, and a full-on production set and crew in order to create a stream of broadcast industry quality that will make people flock to my channel..." school of thought, and the "Huh... I've got a pretty fast laptop and a really good headset..." school of thought. Both are equally valid approaches to streaming, sure, and there are a lot of other disciplines and strategies in-between. The real question is how far you are willing to go, how far do you want to go, and will it be worth it to go that far?

Something streaming and podcasting share in common is that there is no demand for you to convert a room into a broadcasting studio. You do not need a set, lighting equipment, or multiple cameras to stream. You do not have to invest thousands upon thousands of dollars to create the ultimate power stream. (I mean, you could, but before breaking the bank, let's get the basics down, okay?) Streaming is not rocket science. It is incredibly easy to launch a channel, but we're writers. We want i's dotted and t's crossed, right? We're going to spend some quality time filling in the blanks and understanding this platform.

STEP 1 Go to http://twitch.tv and select from the top-right side of your browser window the "Sign Up" option.

 You can still watch Twitch streams without being signed up with the platform. However, if you want to take advantage of the Chat features, you need an account.

STEP 2 Come up with a username for yourself on Twitch, as seen in Figure 8-2.

This is how you will appear in Chat. This can be a nickname you go by, a play on words, or your own name. There can be a lot of different ways you can approach the Username. Just make sure you are not violating any Terms of Service on creating it.

Figure 8-2: Setting up a Twitch channel requires an original username, your birthday, a verified email, and a password that meets the platform's criteria.

Coming up with a Username can be hard. Remember, you want your brand to be as consistent as possible from platform to platform. For example, Tee has been traveling the highways and byways of the Internet under the moniker of "TeeMonster," so Tee tries to use either TeeMonster or TheTeeMonster as his username. This way, people know they have found Tee Morris, author. This is where a brand begins—with a consistent Username.

STEP 3   Create a password or passphrase you can easily recall.

While passwords should be difficult to crack but easy to remember, passphrases are now recommended by cybersecurity experts as upping the difficulty level for being hacked. More characters are involved in passphrases, and if you take something easy like "I am a Fantasy author" and rework it as "!am@Fanta5yauthor" for your password field, you have created a very strong password that meets a platform's criteria.

STEP 4   Enter in your birthday.

Again, this is based on an honor system, but the birthday is there to verify your age and that it is within the Terms of Service as established by Twitch. For more on Twitch's TOS visit https://www.twitch.tv/p/legal/terms-of-service/

STEP 5   Enter a valid email.

This email is where all notifications and any news from Twitch are sent.

STEP 6   After reviewing the Terms of Service and the Privacy Policy, click "Sign Up" to complete the application.

Congratulations! Your Twitch account is now active. Technically, from here, you are ready to start streaming; but there are going to be some additional add-on's you'll need to implement. Presently, the state of your Twitch account is a lot like the state of a Twitter account newly launched where the Profile Picture is the egg, the bio is blank, and the Username is your Twitter handle. When you come across Twitter accounts like that, you can't avoid a hint of skepticism as to how genuine these accounts are. Twitch accounts are no different. And as we stated earlier, we're authors. We need to represent ourselves properly when going live on the Internet. We need to fill in the details that, if you forge ahead without tending to them, will make growth a challenge, ease of use a little elusive, and overall performance lacking. Once you complete your profile, you will not have to worry about them ever again unless you want to update said profile with new information and a re-branding.

Maybe these details feel tedious, but they are the *"Wax on, wax off"* of streaming platforms. Completing these steps will grant you a deeper understanding of the platform.

Completing the Profile

Signing into your newly minted account, your streaming platform is a blank slate where a Profile needs to be completed. Consider your profile as the bio you are writing for your book jacket or a convention program. You want people to know who you are, what you do, and when people can find you online. That's what we are going to build for you right now.

STEP 1   Go to your Twitch account on http://twitch.tv and select from the top-right side of your browser window your Account Status' drop menu. Select "Settings" to enter your Twitch account's Profile, seen in Figure 8-3.

Your Account Status is always visible on the Twitch website. It tells you what is happening on your Channel and shares your activities with friends. You can also go "Invisible" or enable a "Dark Mode" scheme for the Twitch website.

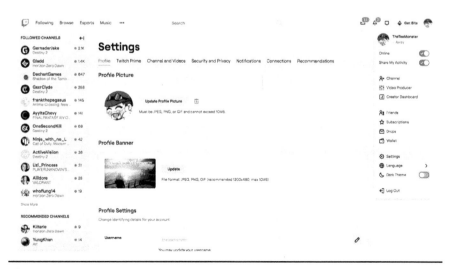

Figure 8-3: Selecting the Settings option will take you to the Profile option of your Twitch account. When completed, it should look something like Tee's, pictured here.

STEP 2   Find a good Profile Picture best representative of you. It can be anything (within reason), but it should be a simple image easily identified at a small size.

Twitch recognizes images in JPEG, PNG, and GIF formats. The dimensions of the image should not exceed 256x256 pixels or be larger than 10MB in file size.

STEP 3   Upload for your "Profile Banner" an image that sets a tone or an atmosphere for your account and Twitch Channel page.

STEP 4   Scroll down to "Profile Settings" and either review or enter in a desired email.

Again, this email is where all notifications and any news from Twitch are sent.

STEP 5   If needed, click on the pencil icon in the "Username" field to edit your Twitch handle.

STEP 6   In the "Display Name" field, edit your Username to appear the way you want it to appear.

In the case of this example, Tee's Username is "theteemonster" but "TheTeeMonster" is how Tee has it displayed.

STEP 7   Scroll down to "Bio" and write up a brief biography of who you are.

STEP 8   Single-click the "Save Changes" button to accept your changes.

Your Profile is all set. When people visit your channel, either online or through the Twitch mobile app, they will see a completed profile. Nothing makes a better first impression than offering the details behind you, your stream, and where people can find your works.

 If you decide that Twitch is not for you, go to *Status > Settings > Disabling Your Twitch Account*. You can follow the link offered to where you can shut your account down.

Setting the Stage: Streaming Software

With the basics of Twitch or whichever streaming platform you have chosen, you will want to install software that will help you stream. You might hear some streamers talk about *Open Broadcaster Software* or *OBS* (http://obsproject.com/), an open source software package that turns your computer and any audio-video components connected to it into a broadcast studio. OBS is a powerful tool and an essential in streaming, but OBS is also a blank slate. Once installed, you launch OBS to have blank screens staring back at you. Nothing really wrong with keeping your stream basic, but on visiting other streamers, you're going to see many streamers have overlays, an image or looped video that offer your stream a little bit of panache. So, instead of struggling to figure out what kind of look you want to create for your stream, turn to *Streamlabs OBS* (http://streamlabs.com) for help.

Figure 8-4: *Streamlabs OBS* offers streamers a one-stop shop for streaming software, statistics tracking, and various add-on's that make your stream dynamic.

While OBS is a blank canvas, Streamlabs OBS (available for Mac and Windows) comes out-of-the-box with a variety of bells and whistles just waiting to be implemented. Streamlabs offers you widgets (small applications that add functionality to your stream) as well as a dashboard that tracks everything from follows to subscriptions to unique views. Streamlabs also offers up overlay templates that range in themes, moods, applications, and colors. With just a few clicks, your stream is transformed from sparse to spectacular.

Incorporating Streamlabs

Streamlabs is both a standalone application and a website, both of which work seamlessly with Twitch, YouTube, and Facebook. In this exercise, we will be working between both the standalone app and the website, and setting up scenes for your stream. While streaming looks incredibly technical, you will discover exactly how quickly we can get set up before we launch our first stream.

STEP 1   Go to http://streamlabs.com and single-click the "Download Streamlabs" button to download the standalone app.

STEP 2   Once the standalone app is downloaded, install and launch Streamlabs OBS. Select your streaming platform and follow the login procedures.

STEP 3   Select your streaming platform and follow the login procedures.

Depending on whether or not you ask your streaming platform to remember login credentials, you may be prompted to perform a full login of username and password. Otherwise, your streaming platform will automatically sync with Streamlabs and take you to your Dashboard.

STEP 4   Set up your computer's Microphone and Camera.

By default, any microphone and camera installed or built into your desktop or laptop computer will be detected. You can plug in external USB microphones and webcams, and select them from drop menus provided.

STEP 5   On reaching the "Optimize" screen, click the "Start" button to allow Streamlabs to look at your Internet settings and computer hardware to apply the best settings for you and your stream.

STEP 6   In the top-left section of the Streamlabs OBS application, single-click the "Themes" option, pictured in Figure 8-5.

Figure 8-5: Streamlabs OBS' Themes section offer you a variety of atmospheres for your stream. All of these looks are customizable, too.

STEP 7   Find a theme for your stream by going to the "Search" bar and type in "free" into the search field. Press the "Return" key and review the search results. Single-click a theme preview to review its various screens or animations.

If a template has in the upper-right corner of its preview an "Animated" level, the template will have some sort of animation to it. On clicking its thumbnail preview to review it, you will see the animation in full.

 You may notice many of the new overlays are labeled with a "Prime" label. With Streamlabs, a Prime account costs $19/month (or $149/annual) and unlocks all themes, along with custom apps and exclusive services. You can still download templates and enjoy analytics with the free edition, but Streamlabs Prime are an investment you should consider if it's worth the cost.

STEP 8   Once you find a theme you like, click the "Install Overlay" button to the top, right-hand side of the preview.

With a template in place, you now need to populate this look with all your incoming video and audio sources in order to get your stream up and running. To transform your computer into a streaming studio comes down to knowing where to click and finding the resources connected to your computer.

Adding an element in your template

Let's say you want to invite people into your creative process and feature on your stream a writing session. We will be using the Streamlabs app to set the scene for your stream, featuring a camera on you and your writing app of choice visible behind you.

STEP 1   Launch your preferred writing application. Have it running in the background.

STEP 2   Return to the Streamlabs app. Click on the "Editor" option in the upper-left corner of the app.

If you have multiple templates loaded into your version of Streamlabs, they can all be accessed from a lower-left menu that will show the current active template.

STEP 3 The template you're working on, if it has a "Starting Soon" scene, will feature an introduction screen. As seen in Figure 8-6, under the name of the template, you will see other Scenes listed.

Scenes are the various stages of your stream. From introduction images to intermission placards, scenes should follow a progress for your Twitch channel.

Figure 8-6: Scenes are different segments of your stream, and in OBS you segue from one to the next whenever you want to go to different segments.

STEP 4 Click on the "Live Scene" scene to see where your stream will happen.

If you have your webcam already plugged in, the template should recognize it straight away.

STEP 5 Look in the "Sources" window (also seen in Figure 8-6) and select the "Background" source. You will see the background image surround itself with a bounding box.

Sources are exactly what they sound like: sources of audio and video needed to make your stream happen. You and Streamlabs are managing all these sources independently of one another, the app behaving something like a mixer.

STEP 6 Single click the "+" to add a source to this "Live Scene" scene. The "Add Source" window comes up. Select the "Window Capture" option, and click the "Add Source" button in the lower-right corner.

STEP 7 In the "Add New Source" field, type "Work Desk" for the name of the source. Click the "Add Source" button.

STEP 8 To the right of the "Window" label, single-click the "Select Option" drop menu and select your writing application's window. Click the "Done" button.

As seen in Figure 8-7, when Streamlabs sees an incoming source, it will drop in the source directly into your scene's layout. We will adjust this in the next step.

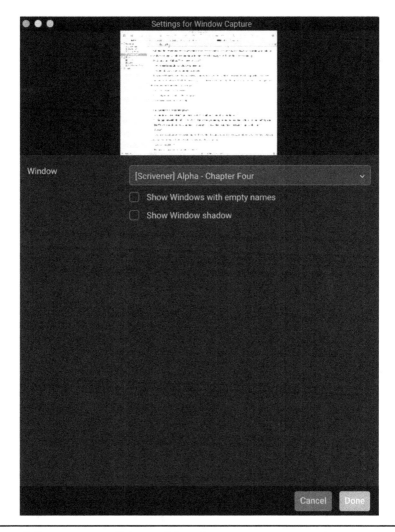

Figure 8-7: Once you tell Streamlabs where a source or signal is coming from, Streamlabs will render the source in your template.

STEP 9 Place your cursor on the bottom-right handle of the word processor's window, and click-and-drag the window to fill one-half of the screen.

STEP 10 In the "Sources" window, click-and-drag "Work Desk" down the list of your sources until it is just above the "Background" source.

In bringing your word processor into this template, you also have an idea of how to customize your template to your own specifications. Let's personalize this template beyond just bringing in your console. Let's put our stream's title in here so people know exactly where they are.

Personalizing Your Template

For this exercise, Tee is using the "Alpha Sections" template. When you are working on your own templates, some of the widgets may be called something different. Other templates may be using different sources or labels, but the steps in making your templates your own should be similar.

STEP 1   Find the header of your template in the "Sources" window and single-click the eyeball to the far right of it. This will hide the layer from view. Single-click the eyeball again to make the source visible.

The two icons to the right of each sources are Source Lock and View/Hide. When a source is locked, it cannot be edited (but can still be removed). Single-clicking the View/Hide option will make a source visible or invisible, although it can still be repositioned and edited.

STEP 2   Where you see the "Stream Label" widget, click on the View/Hide icon to hide it from view. Then lock it.

STEP 3   Where you see the "Text Element" (designated by an "A" icon), single-click and move that in place of the Stream Label.

Each template will be different, but in many of these templates, there will be Stream Labels in place, small widgets that offer up some simple automation between your dashboard and your template. (In the case of the Alpha Sections template, the widget reports who gave the most recent donation to your stream.) Text Elements are just that: static text generated by OBS, most of the time used for headers, footers, and titles. The Text Element here reads "Top Donation" presently.

STEP 4   Double-click the "Text Element" to get to its "Properties" window, seen in Figure 8-8. In the "Text" field, type in a title for your stream. Press the Tab button to see the changes, and click-and-drag the new title within your template to center it either in the layout or within a background graphic.

In the Properties window, you can change other attributes of the text, ranging from font to font size to color.

STEP 5   Click the "Done" button to accept the changes.

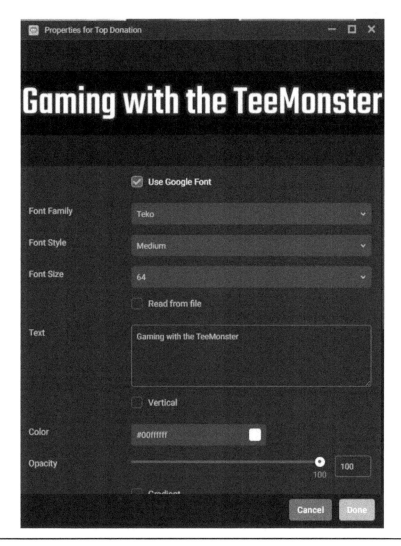

Figure 8-8: Text Elements allow you to personalize this template, giving your stream a simple, unique impression when live.

With the help of Streamlabs OBS, a template can become your own, and what you do to a template can play into your branding as an author. This personalized look to a stream is very common from stream to stream, as streamers want to stand out (and prefer to do so on a tight budget). The more you dive into Streamlabs, the more possibilities for you and your stream reveal themselves. What you want to accomplish and how you want to present yourself on stream is up to you as you are ready to go.

So, I'm ready to stream. Now what?

You have your laptop webcam ready to go and Streamlabs all set up to run. All that remains is to single-click the "Go Live" button and you are streaming. Going live looks easy, but anyone who thinks *"Streaming is easy..."* has never streamed content. With podcasting, you can always edit and remove anything you think is irrelevant or innocuous; but with streaming, you are creating content without a safety net. Whatever you are saying or doing, your content is unfiltered, raw, and uncompromising. And yeah, that can be intimidating.

However, streaming platforms tend to offer categories for streamers in order to give streamers a good place to establish themselves. Many of the categories on platforms are broken down by individual games, so in the *Destiny 2* category, you'll find people talking about or playing Bungie's popular FPSMMORPG. (And if you know what I mean with that, then you got game!) *Fortnite* will have its own category, just make sure to bring some pepper as it can get salty in there. *Overwatch* will host the heroic because the world need heroes. You get the idea. Old games and new will usually have their own category, but what you want to find is the category that welcomes writers. On Twitch, that is known as the *Creative Directory.*

Writers. Cosplayers. Crafters. Photographers. Creative is the corner of Twitch where if you want to teach people Photoshop by doing, where you want to tease your next costuming wonder, or where you want to showcase your work-in-progress, you will find yourself making a home here. All streaming platforms should have a category like this.

Perhaps the love of streaming is better expressed in one of these alternative approaches to Twitch. In exploring these directories, you can see exactly how many opportunities outside of gaming exist for you. And while it is something of a risk putting yourself and your works-in-progress out there for evaluation (because this is the Internet and people will evaluate your work), streaming can make the profession of a writer feel less solitary.

Streaming can also be a great platform for your podcast. Using the platform, you can record your podcast with a live audience, take questions in real time, and offer "bonus content" that does not necessarily make it on the final episode that hits your RSS feed. So, while we have you set up for a writing session, you can easily set up Streamlabs to record your podcast, offering yourself a "backup" in case your audio recording software hiccups.

If you are beginning to think that streaming is something of an upgrade from podcasting, it is. Like any upgrade, though, the extent of what you invest in streaming ranges from which solution best suits you to how far your budget travels down the streaming rabbit hole.

Digging Deep for an Audience of Zero

Perhaps the hardest thing to see when you are streaming is to look at your audience count and see a fat goose egg staring back at you. The analytics are always present, and when you see there is no one watching, it is incredibly difficult to not appear disappointed. *"Why am I doing this again?"* you might find yourself asking. How exactly do you stream when no one's watching?

At times like that, you have to find what drives you and push on through. Otherwise, you will never grow from where you are presently: the beginning of a new platform.

Your stream comes from you. Successful streaming comes from the drive and the passion you put into it. Numbers will go up and down, that's the nature of streaming, but your performance on stream should be no different in front of a stream of one or a stream of one hundred and fifty. Whether it be Twitch, YouTube, or some other platform—regardless of how many are watching—you should take a lot of pride in the fact that you are in a routine of creating content and sharing your passion with the world. Don't go quiet. Keep talking. Share your thoughts and opinions on pop culture, the state of your short story or novel, and what you are learning from the interaction with your community.

Yeah, maybe statistics hurt; but if you are having fun, there's a good chance word will get out that your stream is one to watch.

What you have here is a very basic approach to streaming. If you sample streaming and find you want know more about your options, the accessories you need, and additional strategies concerning the kind of content you can create, take a look at another title of Tee's from the For Dummies people, *Twitch for Dummies*. In the various chapters of that title, details are covered, and a brave new world is presented to you. Go exploring.

IX: ADDITIONAL OPTIONS

PLATFORMS THAT BREAK THE CONVENTIONS

T he social media space is always evolving, and new platforms are constantly springing up to demand the attention of readers and writers alike.

Some platforms generate wild interest for a few days or weeks, before being cast aside; some new ones offer features or conveniences that the old ones do not and are taken into the fold.

Authors should always keep their eyes on the social media horizon to see what is newly available, but before they sign up at any site, they must evaluate it. Does the site offer new audiences? Is it reaching more people than already established sites? Is there some new aspect of marketing that can be achieved with them that others do not? In particular, are groups of readers gathering in these new places?

The platforms we cover here are not as mainstream as Facebook, Twitter, or Instagram, but these are networks that are popular with authors, where writers are found frequently, and where they can sometimes find a new and unique angle to promote their work or just be themselves.

Discord

One platform quickly on the rise when it comes to communications and community development is *Discord* (https://discordapp.com/). At first glance, Discord looks and sounds like Skype on steroids. It is a robust, stable communications platform available as a browser application, a stand-alone desktop application, and a mobile app for both smartphones and tablets. Discord has a lot to offer a writer:

- Text Chat
- Private Text Messaging
- Link Sharing
- Media Sharing
- Audio Chat (Group and Private)
- Video Chat (Group and Private)
- News Feeds

But what makes this platform "out of the ordinary" for writers is its close association to gaming. One of many reasons this platform is so closely associated with gaming is due in part to its founder, Jason Citron, a founder of a social gaming platform for mobile games and a game development studio. His development team introduced Discord in May 2015 as a communications alternative and it quickly gained popularity with eSports gamers and Twitch.tv hosts.

So, when it comes to gaming, Discord is an essential for games comms. For writers, it has a potential for building an online clubhouse for readers of your works and always looking for the latest podcast you're appearing on or interview going live.

Getting Started

There is a lot to getting Discord fully operational, so we will keep it to three basics you should know about the platform:

- Launching a server
- Setting up channels for discussions
- Posting text messages

With an explanation of those basics, if you think Discord is a platform you want to explore, take a deep dive with Discord for Dummies. Tee gets down and dirty with the app and takes you through a variety of finer details.

Let's go on and set you up with an account first, applying some of the concepts we have been learning and reviewing throughout this book.

STEP 1   Launch your browser of choice and go to http://www.discordapp.com.

STEP 2   Discord will offer you two options: *Download for your OS* or *Open Discord in Your Browser.* Go on and select the "Open Discord in Your Browser" option.

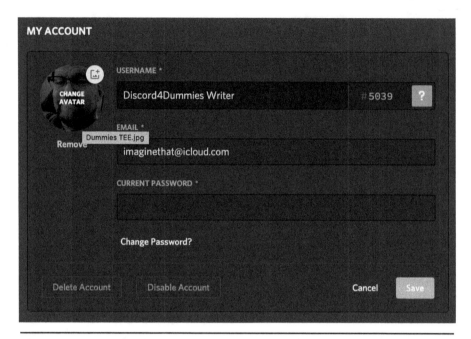

Figure 9-1: When coming up with a username on Discord, remember to make sure to build on the brand you're building for yourself.

STEP 3   When asked to enter a Username for yourself, create one matching or close to your other social media platforms. On hitting the arrow button to the right, you will be asked to verify you're not an automated program or bot.

STEP 4   Choose your preferred method of verification and follow the steps to assure Discord that you are in fact a real person.

STEP 5   You are then asked to either set up your server or jump into Discord. Click the "Get Started" option.

STEP 6   In the "Create Your Server" option, come up with a name for your server. Create a server name and select the server region closest to your location in the world.

When you join Discord, you create what is called a server. This is your own private corner of Discord, and you decide how public your chat will be. If you don't like what you initially name your server, don't worry — you can always change it later in the "Settings" section of your server.

STEP 7   You must now claim the server as your own with a valid email and password.

You will be sent an email asking you to claim the server, making you its Moderator, the one in charge of the whole operation.

Figure 9-2: Creating a server on Discord is simple. Establish a region from where your server operates, then give your server a name.

STEP 8   When you claim your server via email confirmation, you are live on Discord! Once you verify, return to the Discord browser window.

STEP 9   Go to the top-left of the app where you see your server name. Click on the arrow pointing down to get the drop-down menu and select "Server Settings" from the options listed.

STEP 10   "Server Overview" offers you the ability to load up an icon for your server. If you are working on your branding, use the same image you are using throughout your social media.

STEP 11   Scroll to the bottom of "Server Settings" to click the "Save Changes" button, then hit the ESC key to return to Discord.

When you launch a Discord server, there is very little to see. It's a bit of a desolate landscape on a digital front. So where exactly do we go from here? We need to set up topics of discussion. Once you offer places for people to meet and chat, you'll start seeing traffic on your server.

Establishing Channels in Your Discord

Offering people channels is how conversations get started on Discord. Each channel is like breaking the ice at a party with a question. What's on your editorial desk at present? What are you reading? Where are your favorite places to eat? Did you binge-watch anything good on Netflix?

All of these questions serve as the basis of channels on your Discord.

STEP 1   In the left-hand side of Discord, find your text and voice channels. Under Text Channels, click on the "Add Channel" option (a large + sign located to the right of the Text Channels label) to create a new channel.

Channels are dedicated topics that you want to share with your followers and subscribers. Here are a few ideas for what your server can feature:

- WIP
- The Latest (news on book deals, launching a podcast, etc.)
- Current Reads
- Appearances
- Movies
- Pet Selfies

This is one of the best attributes of Discord. It offers you the ability to sort and organize your interests.

STEP 2   In the "Create Text Channel" window, go on and label your new channel a topic relevant to your interests, and make sure "Text Channel" is the Channel Type selected. Leave the Private Channel option turned off.

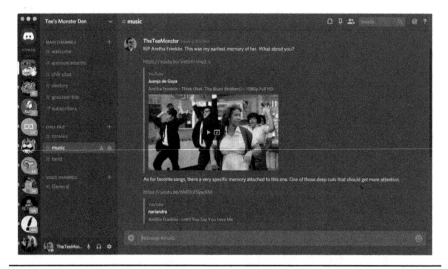

FIGURE 9-3: Categories, or *Channels*, help organize your Discord Server, assisting visitors in finding quickly what they want to talk about.

STEP 3   Single-click the "Create Channel" button.

STEP 4   Repeat Steps 2–4 to create other channels of interest.

STEP 5   Right-click on the TEXT CHANNELS header, and select the "Edit Category" option.

STEP 6   Give the Text Channels category the new title of "Main Channels" in the Category Name field. Single-click the green "Save" button.

STEP 7   Click-and-drag the channels of your Discord Server into their appropriate categories.

Your Discord is now live, and we have topics of discussion. Cool. This is a great first step. Now, how do you create content for these topics?

Putting a Post Together
Let's say that you want to share on #the-latest channel a YouTube video of someone reviewing your book. How would we go about doing this?

STEP 1   Go to http://youtube.com and look for media (in this case, the book review) you want to share.

STEP 2   At the YouTube link, single-click the Share option. From the window, single-click the Copy option. Look for a notification at the bottom-left of the browser window that you copied the URL.

STEP 3   Return to your Discord server. Find the channel where you want to post the URL.

STEP 4   Single-click the channel you want to post in, and in the "Message [#name-of-channel]" field, type out the following with the copied YouTube link:

This went live this week and it thrills me to hear what people think. What about you? Let me know your thoughts here, or in a review of your own!

[paste YouTube link here]

STEP 5   Single-click the Enter key.

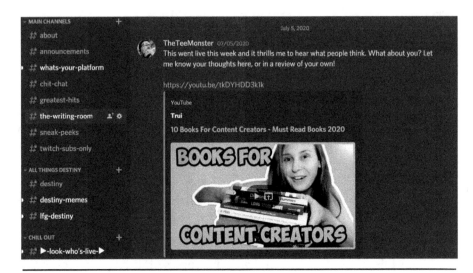

Figure 9-4: In Discord, it is easy to share links, images, and YouTube clips in channels.

Pictured in Figure 9-4 is a message and accompanying URL, posted in the channel. A preview is rendered of the link, and you can either watch the clip in Discord or click on a provided link to go to YouTube.

Discord supports several kinds of media:

- URLs
- JPG and PNG images
- Animated GIFs
- MP3 files
- M4V and MP4 files
- Emojis and Emotes

Yeah, suddenly the Internet feels a bit bigger. Discord is definitely a long-game strategy. You don't simply throw a switch and — boom — you have a community. You have to build it, set aside time to cultivate it, and continue to nurture the community there. To find out more about exactly what you can do on this platform, take a look at Tee's deep dive into the platform entitled *Discord for Dummies.*

reddit

And now for a quick look at another communication platform that you should pay attention to as a writer: *reddit.* Reddit (http://www.reddit.com) is best described as a social networking service where users can submit content, then said content is voted up or down by a network of users. Creating an account at reddit.com is easy enough to do, but navigating this platform could seem a little intimidating, at first. If you are old enough to remember online bulletin boards, then you are going to be right at home on reddit. However, unlike the 1990s, reddit is massive and divided into impossible to count the number of subreddits—topics any user can create. With so much content, it can feel a little daunting at first.

As an author venturing into reddit, you should stick to the books subreddit at first. This is our familiar area after all. Remember this is a moderated subreddit, so look on the right-hand sidebar to take note of the rules for participating in this community. The books subreddit is one of the most populated places readers can go to discuss books. Forty thousand new subscribers come on board every week. Books even has its own book group, which must be the largest anywhere at twelve thousand members. Just imagine trying to get that many folks into a room at once.

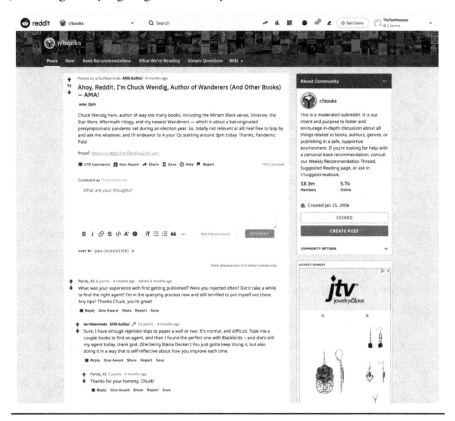

Figure 9-5: The forum-based platform *reddit* (http://www.reddit.com) offers writers a great place to talk to readers and writers from all backgrounds about how you approach bylines and deadlines.

From this subreddit, you can drill down if you like, but since we are concentrating on the social aspect of these other platforms, let's check out one of the more popular and allowable ways for authors to use reddit.

Ask Me Anything (AMA)

AMAs are quickly becoming the go-to way for authors to spread the word about their books and to connect with readers who may have already read it. AMAs are not restricted to authors—even the American president has done one—but they can be fun and informative. You are basically creating a worldwide chance for readers, both potential and otherwise, to ask you questions.

Carefully read over the AMA FAQs found at http://www.reddit.com/r/IAmA/wiki/index to make sure you know the procedure for both requesting an AMA and creating one.

You know, all this talk about social media, its capabilities, and what an author can do with it has certainly left me parched. I could use a drink…

A Social's Social: Untappd, Vivino, and Distiller

Authors can close deals, create new contacts, and expand leads for future writing gigs just about anywhere, but perhaps the best wheeling-and-dealing happens at the bar. Occasionally dubbed "BarCon," a lot of networking happens in the conference hotel's bar. Social media comes into play when you are off the clock at a convention, expo, or conference, its innovative ways connect you with other writers, readers, and the world, but these networks exist simply to provide writers a place to share a frosty beverage or a celebratory round once a contract is signed or a day of book signings are done.

Untappd (http://untappd.com) is a network built for those who love beer. Be it a porter, a pilsner, or an IPA, Untappd connects you with ice-cold brewskis and the breweries behind them. The network is accessed either on a website or a mobile application, and offers you access to Untappd's beer database comprised of mainstream breweries to up-and-coming microbreweries to home brewers you may meet on your travels. At the core of the app are the reviews. When your first round arrives, you search for your beer in the Search bar across the top. Once you tap your beer from the list of offered brews, you select "Check-In" and are offered a field where you can:

- Type in a brief review (Best reviews are around 150 characters)
- Add a photo of what you are drinking (or who you are drinking with, as Tee did here with author Lauren B. Harris)
- Rate your brew
- Add your location

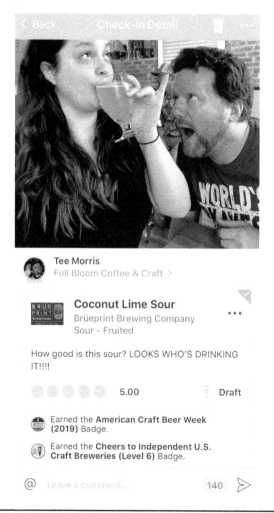

Figure 9-6: When you want to celebrate that latest deadline accomplishment or new contract, or share a beer with another writerly friend, put together a post on *Untappd* (http://untappd.com).

But what if beer isn't your thing? That's okay as Untappd also includes in its database ciders and meads as well.

For wine lovers, *Vivino* (http://vivino.com) is the app of choice. Much like its ale-driven counterpart, Vivino allows you the ability to rate and review wines; but it's how you find a wine in the Vivino network that is particularly clever. Point your camera at the wine bottle's label and take a photo. Vivino will scan its database and find the wine you currently have in front of you, or allow you to enter all of the information about this wine (vineyard, category, vintage, country of origin) along with your own comments. This wine lover's network also scans wine lists, offering reviews and notes from the glasses and bottles featured, price lists for wines you may want to stock your own cellars with, a "location search" that shows you what wines are near your current location, and your own statistics—what you've tried, what you've liked and what you didn't.

Now that we have our beer snobs and wine connoisseurs covered, we will turn to an app that would have sparked the interest of rogues and rascals like Ernest Hemingway, Raymond Chandler, and Hunter S. Thompson.

Distiller (http://distiller.com) covers scotch, bourbon, rye, and other kinds of whiskey. The app and website grant its members access to both trending and recent whiskey rated by the network and the "Tasting Table," which is Distiller's own inner circle of experts and enthusiasts who come together to offer recommendations for what you should be enjoying by the fire pit or after dinner. Wish lists can be built alongside your Collection and your Top Shelf, all of which are shared on your profile.

These are clever apps, sure, but this book is about social media for writers. How can authors take advantage of these uncommon networks? It's a worthwhile question, as these networks don't necessarily lend themselves to promotion of your books.

Your brand, however, is a different matter.

If you visit TeeMorris.com, you will often see him refer to himself as "Beer Snob," a self-proclaimed title that Tee is proud to wear. With many check-ins from Untappd, Tee has made his love and appreciation of microbrews a part of his brand.

But when it comes to posting on these networks, authors can add a casual flavor to their social media platforms.

Instant content for other social networks. Untappd, Vivino, and Distiller all offer integration with larger networks like Facebook and Twitter. With the incorporation of photos, these apps offer your networks dynamic content that can easily spark discussions and other recommendations that you can explore at other social events. These platforms can also offer you a new way to connect with potential interests that your readers may have—

remember, your readers want to get to know you. Untappd, Vivino, and Distiller provide new and varied content to your various platforms, and variety is essential to success.

Dining recommendations for your area or areas new to you. Whether you want to offer an impromptu meeting place for fans or are looking for a place to try on the road, these barfly apps can automatically access your location to see what people are saying about featured labels—be they local, international, or just new to you. These apps also work as a kind of *Urbanspoon* or *OpenTable* (both apps designed to recommend dining options in your immediate area) for various restaurants, brewpubs, or even vineyards, cideries, and distilleries.

Getting to know your fellow authors. We originally met Elizabeth Bear at a steampunk event in 2013, but it was 2014 when Tee connected with her on Untappd. Since then he has shared quite a few toasts and notes with the acclaimed science fiction and fantasy author. Appreciators and aficionados of beer, wine, and spirits love to exchange notes on what they are drinking and where they are drinking it. It's fun to do, and you get to know the tastes of your friends who are dedicated to the literary pursuits. With Distiller's ability to share wish lists across other networks, a bottle of a desired or favorite label makes for a wonderful gift.

Sharing a Celebration or a Quiet Moment with Fans. Readers love to feel a connection with their favorite author. The limits of how much you want to share, as we have said before, are up to you; but fans do appreciate when authors share images of toasts and celebrations. You can be sitting by a fire pit with a single malt in hand or toasting with other authors to a recent award, accomplishment, or appearance—sharing the round through these apps can create a "bonding" moment with your readers.

A dear friend of ours, social media professional Megan Enole, has been known to say, "Never forget the social in social media." If these are words to live by (and they are), then the thing that makes these unique networks so much fun is also the thing that's so good for writers and their platforms—Discord, reddit, and Untappd are all about being social. When you want to celebrate, when you want to unwind, or when you want to suggest a favorite drink, these platforms are off-the-beaten-path for many writers, but just as powerful in their reach as Facebook, Twitter, or Instagram. As you can see, there is not lack of social media for an author to take advantage of. Once again, it is all about finding out where your audience is and making yourself available there.

Have a look at what these platforms can do for you in getting the word out about your next byline, and see where these possibilities will lead you.

X: CONTENT MARKETING

Promoting Through Others

L ogic would tell you that investing in some kind of online advertising, whether you pay to show up on other blogs, boost Pages and posts on Facebook, or engage with other social media platforms, would be the easiest way to get the word out about you and your books. This is traditional marketing at its core: Paying for the platform in order to reach your audience. This is how marketing has worked since its inception, and if you hear the story behind those who inspired the TV show *Mad Men*, you'll find that marketing is a funny and slightly sneaky business of manipulation, public relations, and showmanship. You have to convince your audience, be they loyal fans or potential readers, that your book is the book to read, that your series is the next big thing, and that you are a writer to watch. This is how marketing works and has worked for decades.

Follow that same logic with social media, though, and you are more likely to win the lottery than to propel your book up the rankings of Amazon and the bestseller lists at *The New York Times*.

Social media, and those who have mastered it, never forget what is at its core: real people. So many authors forget the social aspect of social media. You need to make a connection with your audience and establish yourself not only as a skilled storyteller but also as an expert on what you are writing about. You need to establish trust with your audience, which, to an extent, traditional marketing does, but what traditional marketing fails to understand is that social media is not for bombarding an audience with the same message over and over again (as we have seen numerous times with authors on Twitter saying some version of *"Buy my book. It's awesome!"* in their feed). Doing so simply drives a social media audience away.

You might notice that those same authors who continuously promote their books have an astounding number of followers—some even reach the tens of thousands. Experience has shown us that most of those followers are purchased. Again, it's a sign of traditional marketing mishandling social media, as it's all about the numbers in traditional marketing. Marketing and social media, though, have found a happy medium, and there is a good possibility that you have been practicing it already, provided you are online trying out the different platforms. Content marketing takes a very different approach in that it promotes through the content of others. In a sense, you are promoting your own works by showcasing someone else's related work.

Perhaps now you may be thinking "Wait a minute. I'm promoting myself by promoting others. That doesn't make sense!" Content marketing follows a different strategy. Instead of your platform centering only on your book, it centers on your interests.

On our own *Ministry of Peculiar Occurrences* Facebook Page, we feature links about our books, special events where we will be appearing, and links to our newsletter. Our Page (as well as our other platforms like Twitter, Tumblr, and Instagram) also offers news on those who write for *Tales from the Archives*, promotes other steampunk events across the country and around the world, and shares links about steampunk music, fashion, and entertainment. We even feature other authors and their works, especially if the authors are part of our *Tales from the Archives* podcast.

This may seem backwards, especially when we promote other authors' books, but in content marketing you are establishing your blog and your social networks as reliable resources for your subject matter. In the case of the *Ministry of Peculiar Occurrences*, our expertise is steampunk. What kind of content do our various platforms cover?

- Steampunk
- Dieselpunk
- Atompunk (sometimes called Retropunk)
- Victorian history
- Science fiction, fantasy, and horror

It is incredible how many different topics can directly tie in with your work.

Content marketing allows you to find other voices in your profession who share your interest. You can then share with your readers, fans, and fellow writers terrific resources that inspire you to work harder and write better. You will want to read and research whatever you share or syndicate on your website to be sure the article you're sharing is coming from a credible, reliable source. What we consider the "work" in content marketing is making sure we stand by the resources we share. That may take some time spent reviewing what's out there, but when you see traffic coming to your blog, your Instagram account, or your Twitch channel, it is a rewarding sight indeed. You're establishing trust with your audience and building a reputation as a reliable resource in a shared interest.

How Does Promoting Other Really Work for You?

How exactly content marketing works as a promotion tool is still difficult for some authors to grasp. Traditional marketing is all about repetition. It becomes a bombardment of advertising, and an increase in Twitter followers is perceived as successful. But is it? Are people interacting with you on your networks? Are you talking with your virtual street team, or are you merely broadcasting the same message over and over again, eventually turning your signal into noise?

Figure 10-1: Tor.com, the official website of Tor Books, does more than promote their own works and authors; but provides a hub for all things Science Fiction, Fantasy, and Horror.

With content marketing, you establish your name and your works as part of a larger brand, and your website is the place online to get the latest news on your interests. Content marketing begins when you discover an article that speaks to you and you know sharing it would resonate with your audience. Once you share it, your audience receives new content. In turn, the origin of the resource—maybe a blog like Boing Boing, a podcast like *Writing Excuses*, or the Instagram of an author like Piper J. Drake or Bill Blume—receives traffic from your audience. This sharing benefits both sides, and the person receiving the new traffic, if savvy, will drive traffic to you in return. This reciprocal approach to marketing builds audiences and communities; the more you share, the stronger your reputation within these circles.

A great example of content marketing at work is Tor.com. A science fiction publisher, Tor delves into far more than just books and its latest releases. Tor.com features columns from authors (even those outside of its catalog) talking about the genre, writing, and media of past and present. The blog also has sections dedicated to upcoming special events (including conventions and expos), art from content creators of all backgrounds, and various discussion threads by readers and writers from around the world. Tor.com has established itself as a go-to resource for relevant content in science fiction, fantasy, and horror, all the while promoting its own brand.

 We talk a bit about attribution throughout the book and in more detail in the Best Practices chapter, but considering how many people completely forget (or ignore) this little detail, it bears repeating: Just because you find something on the Internet doesn't mean it's yours. If you see a post—be it from another author or just a friend—don't turn it into a shareable meme and claim it for yourself. When someone provides content relevant to you (and your audience), make sure you give credit where it is due. A lack of attribution only hurts your online reputation. Avoid violating this rule at all costs.

What Content to Look for in Content Marketing

When heading out into the wide expanse of the Internet for content, it is a real challenge to find exactly what you are looking for. What is content that makes you think "Oh yeah, this would be great for my audience!" It may sound easy—just find some good articles on a blog here or a Facebook Page there—but you actually need a strategy if you want to provide the best content for your audience.

Reliable Sources

You've heard it said again and again, but before you repost anything, it is always a good idea to dig deep into a Web page, blog, or social media link. Resources like Tor.com, io9.com, *The Washington Post*, Mashable, and *Huffington Post* tend to be rock solid in their research and reliability (but no, they are not perfect). It's when you go to personal blogs or websites that you'll need verification, particularly if you're not familiar with them. You really want to be certain that the news and commentary offered is something that you can stand behind and say, "Yes, we agree." Take a moment to check the resources you're not acquainted with and assure that proper attribution is given.

Current Sources

Try to syndicate and share advice and tips that are relevant. Think of how much publishing has changed since the introduction of the Kindle. How relevant would advice on formatting books for e-readers be right now if it was published in 2015 or earlier? Tech news, in particular, has an extremely limited shelf life. You want to find stories, advice, and reviews that date back no more than a year or two, unless it is evergreen content or content that shows "how some things never change" (or "how things have changed since ..."). The more up to date your resources, the more relevant your site or platform becomes.

Figure 10-2: When you share resources in your content marketing plan, keep your sources not only reliable but current, like *Forbes* (http://forbes.com) who are always keeping news and developments up-to-date.

Creative Sources

The content you can share, be it your own or content from another source, should stimulate or motivate your creativity. Inspirational quotes or nuggets of advice that inspire you would also make for great content to share. If you are sharing another resource, check its origin just to be sure it is not a site that promotes ideas or agendas contrary to your own. You will also want to check the validity of quotes. Sometimes quotes are paraphrased or can't clearly be attributed to one person. Sharing comical images, such as memes, can be great for your Web traffic.

 Another note concerning attribution and memes: Some less-than-scrupulous authors take memes from other sites and apply Photoshop to remove the original attribution (usually a website in a lower corner), or they simply crop out the URL of a meme's origins. Even reproducing a meme seen elsewhere is a questionable practice. In other words, it is never wise to scrape another's content—and that includes re-branding it for your own use.

Appropriate Sources

This tip tends to be rather tricky to define because everyone's idea of what is appropriate is different. If you are engaging in content marketing for edgy or sensational titles, then your content may reflect that. You define "appropriate" content for your blog or site, but remember the content you share reflects you, your brand, and your titles. There is no consistency between when readers "give a pass" to authors and their opinions and when readers hold authors accountable. Therefore, when you post content outside of your brand, your series, or your title, and that content expresses political, religious, sensitive, or edgy humor or topics, keep in mind that the content reflects on you—possibly in ways that you may not like. Set boundaries for yourself, and remember that your boundaries may still be out of bounds for some. Be ready to face pushback if you stray out of your brand's comfort zone.

When working with content marketing, you will want to be patient and consistent. There is no magic bullet, no sure-fire formula, and no fool proof way to gain traction overnight, so you have to find a schedule and a pattern, and stick with it in order to build your platform.

Figuring out what works with your audience can be frustrating. Sometimes it will be the post about your book that will result in traffic and numbers, and sometimes a post from another source that caught your eye will drive traffic. What matters in the end is the quality of your content. If you provide your Page, your Instagram, or your blog followers with quality content, and you turn your platform into a go-to source for reliable resources and fantastic media, you will establish a connection between you, your audience, and your work. When you've established yourself as an authority on a topic, people will find your work.

When Content Marketing Goes Bad

Content marketing can be a positive, community-building strategy for any business, whether you're a writer, editor, publisher, or even a literary agent. However, some writers and social media mavericks regard any online content as free for use, free of responsibility or credit. This unethical approach to sharing content, as we have mentioned before, is known as scraping. Similar to when blog content is syndicated without attribution, scraping occurs when the origins of the content are removed and posters tag the accompanying content with their own page, giving the appearance that the shared content is original.

Another dark side of content marketing is establishing a social media platform with only one goal: collecting thousands upon thousands of Likes, Favorites, and other statistics in order to eventually sell the account to the highest bidder. Along with scraping content, the following is a list of ways some of these bogus accounts collect massive numbers:

- Meme generation
- Quizzes
- Photographs and artwork (posted without attribution)
  "Follow-for-follow" campaigns

Figure 10-3: Along with using artwork and characters without permission, vendors specializing in *data mining*—gathering personal information for potential advertisers—sell their audiences to the highest bidder.

Social networks attempt to crack down on these unethical accounts, usually through the diligence of their users. Keeping tabs on billions of users, however, can be a daunting task. When putting together your brand's platform, strategy remains key in a successful social media campaign, but it is good to remain aware of what bad content marketing looks like. It is easy to lose yourself in social media's numbers game, and while it may appear that these questionable tactics work in building up your following, quality should always trump quantity. Aim to provide essential, relevant content that will bring people to your Page and keep them coming back, and you will make a strong support system of your platform.

Content marketing that's carried out with the right strategy and execution can prove to be a better way of promoting your book. By building your brand around a community comprised of more than just readers, you have the potential to build a network of artists, musicians, and other writers, all of whom offer their own platforms as sources of promotion. Be patient and consistent, and make sure you use all of your networks to build a community around your quality content.

XI: BEST PRACTICES IN SOCIAL MEDIA

STRATEGIES APPLICABLE TO ANY PLATFORM

Social media has become a great machine of communication and innovation. While some may consider it a distraction, these networks have become entwined in our everyday lives in a deep and real way. So how do you use that network to share your work.

There is no magic bean, no sure-fire way to make magic happen, but in social media hard work, respect, knowledge of the medium, and a solid strategic plan will certainly help you. Here are some finals words of wisdom, that will serve you well across all the platforms you wish to use.

Create an Editorial Calendar

Remember: Content is king. From the early days of the Internet to today, that still remains true. Quality content is what people want from a blog, a podcast, or a social network.

However, content must go in partnership with consistency. There needs to be a rhythm or set schedule to your updates online. A writer cannot simply slap content—even good content—on their blog, Facebook, or elsewhere, and then walk away from it for months on end. One or two, or even a smattering of posting of excellent content will not make much of a splash if it does come at regular intervals that the consumer can rely on. It's about being consistent in posting.

Set a schedule for specific days or be frequent when you post. The best way to manage all of your content, whether blogging, Facebook posting, tweeting, or everything in between, is to set up an editorial calendar that lists when and where you will be posting new content.

Your calendar should list topics or reoccurring columns you are posting on your blog, as well as where you are posting and on which days. (For example, your calendar should show that you're posting on blogs and Facebook on Mondays and Wednesdays, while Tuesday and Friday are dedicated to Twitter and Pinterest.) Once you have a realistic editorial calendar set up, make sure you stick with it and fulfill the schedule. Map out how many posts will be original content that markets your work, and how many will be informational content.

But your schedule shouldn't be forever locked in stone. Allow your editorial calendar flexibility for when fresh topics and news crops up. You want to be able to take advantage of them, not necessarily for the sake of traffic (although some people do that) but for when you really have something to say about a current topic or trend. People will be looking for keywords, so make SEO work for you by keeping up on what is going on in publishing, writing, and your area of expertise.

Content managed in an organized fashion is much less intimidating for an author to approach, than a slapdash approach. With a proper editorial calendar and different outlets featuring daily postings, it will soon become habit rather than a rushed afterthought.

Think Before You Post

When you build a platform in social media, you are building a brand. Your brand reflects what you produce, broadcasting your reliability as an author to your audience. It takes a long time to create a solid brand, but just one ill-thought-out blog post, one impulsive tweet, or one snarky caption on Pinterest can inflict a lot of damage. Sarcastic statements and other attempts of comedy can backfire in a big way so it is a good idea to look over an update before it goes live and try to see it objectively, asking yourself "Could this be taken the wrong way?" Chances are, it could be; but that doesn't mean you shouldn't post it. Just mentally prepare for the blowback if there is any. Comedy can be hard on social media.

What is not difficult to find, on the other hand, is controversy. You may be impassioned by something in the headlines, an exchange on Twitter, or an image in Instagram, but before you let your passionate support for a cause fly, ask yourself "Is this argument worth undertaking?" Do you really understand both sides of the debate? Is the time you spend replying and addressing opposing viewpoints affordable? Or are you on a deadline and want to stay focused? If you do step into the middle of a heated debate, are you prepared to face a negative reaction?

You may have heard the terms thrown around often but what exactly is a *troll* on the Internet? Not far from their literary counterparts who lurk under bridges to snatch travelers unexpectedly, trolls lurk in the darkest corners of the Internet either looking for arguments to kick up or insults to let fly. Trolls care very little about making a point on either side of an argument. They care more about how much they can rattle people, especially the host of a blog, podcast, or platform. This means the insults can go from juvenile to sensational to deeply personal.

Remember that you have the final say for who says what on your platform. Make sure to take advantage of blocking features, and above all—don't feed the trolls. There is a reason you have "Block" functions in many of the social networking tools covered in this book. The best way to handle a troll: block and walk away.

In fact, anytime you look at a post that you've written, stop and ask yourself "Would I be okay sharing this with a roomful of strangers?" Even though your network calls themselves "friends" or "followers," the truth is your network does not know you as well as you think. Consider consequences with any update you are about to make before it becomes necessary to break glass and push the red button in case of emergencies.

Finding the Positive

Going along with thinking before posting, here's another good rule before hitting send: Be positive.

As a professional using social media, you really don't have the luxury of being able to whine, complain, or go on rants. (Granted the occasional rant can be fun, depending on the topic. Pip got good traction on her blog when she went on a tongue-in-cheek rave on the trend in book covers that had lead characters with their heads cropped out.) Many authors have built a community around their reinforcing, positive message, be it in writing advice or lessons learned while on the road with their books. People have enough cynicism and negativity in their regular lives. They may not want to hear it from authors—especially ones they want to enjoy the company of social media with.

Figure 11-1: Positive posts may not get the same kind of traffic as the sensational or negative posts, but they do a lot to further your brand.

So, focus on lessons learned and what you want to share. Be charming, funny, witty and sharing. Such qualities will take you far with readers.

Participate in Blog Tours

These are events that, if managed properly, can be a fantastic way to introduce your words to new readers and, in a reciprocal manner, introduce new bloggers to your readership. These events also give you a good backlist of evergreen content. Blog posts such as these can be easily overhauled, updated, and then repurposed for your own blog. If you are repurposing blog posts, you should wait roughly six months in order to give the original column some exclusivity where it first appears. It's the friendliest thing to do to maintain good relationships with other bloggers.

The way blog tours work is that you appear as a guest blogger across a network of blogs—blogs that cover a variety of topics or perhaps share a common theme. Other bloggers, once or twice a week, in turn, appear on your blog, sharing topics they would like to cover or ones you have previously suggested. To make tours a success for everyone involved, the content bloggers deliver to one another should be:

- Original
- Unique from blog to blog
- Fall within the 500-1,000 word count

Some bloggers may fail to promptly post others' contributions, but if all participants contribute on schedule, your evergreen content will grow substantially. This gives you many options for posts that can later be repurposed for your own blog or for future guest postings.

 When you are on a blog tour, you are expected to generate original posts for each stop. Do not create one blog post and offer it as your sole contribution. When embarking on a blog tour, you are committing to your tour hosts new, original, unique content. Make sure you meet that commitment.

Create Quality Content

Content can come from a variety of sources, but your content should always be quality. What is defined as quality content? It's subjective, but quality content should be clear, concise, edited, and well researched. There is a popular opinion that posting content for content's sake is what matters, not the actual worth of your content; but all of your posts are important because they are a reflection of your work.

So, what do people look for in quality content?

Timeliness. When news pertaining to your business hits the headlines, you have roughly twenty-four to forty-eight hours to write, edit, and post a blog post. At the latest, you have within a week (roughly five days) to blog your own commentary on a topic. At the time of breaking news, people are specifically searching out articles and angles on this topic. By tapping into the timeliness of a news story, you increase your chances of other blogs picking up and syndicating your blog post. Wait too long, and the opportunity to take advantage of the story and drive traffic will be lost.

Cross Promotion. Once a blog post goes live, Facebook and Twitter should be the beginning of your promotion. While there are automated posting tools like the WordPress plug-in Social that broadcast updates on your blog, these postings feel rather cold. Following a flow chart (similar to the editorial calendar), you should compose an original, accompanying post or tweet and then add it to your latest blog post. This lets your various networks know that while there is crossover between your channels, you are handling each account and keeping content fresh.

Cross Referencing. Remember that your words reflect directly on you, so it is a good idea to link your references back to your blog posts. Sharing resources and linking back to them are terrific discussion starters, as commenters will ask more about the sources or spark debates on the resources cited. Sharing links may also encourage traffic to your own website, depending on the generosity and the respect of the referred website. Either way, cross-referencing is a terrific tactic for generating traffic around your blog.

Be Visual When Possible

Nothing attracts attention like a good image. Users consistently interact with images more than text-only posts, across all platforms. Some platforms are particularly focused on images—Pinterest and Tumblr—but posts and tweets will get more eyeballs on your content with the addition of an image. Don't forget: *Images in blog posts rule!*

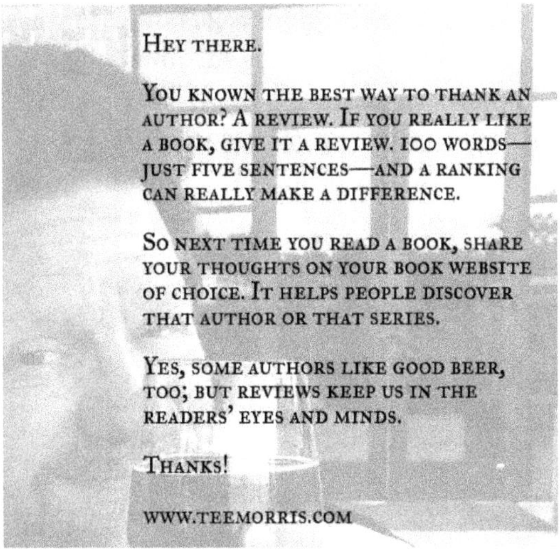

HEY THERE.

YOU KNOWN THE BEST WAY TO THANK AN AUTHOR? A REVIEW. IF YOU REALLY LIKE A BOOK, GIVE IT A REVIEW. 100 WORDS— JUST FIVE SENTENCES—AND A RANKING CAN REALLY MAKE A DIFFERENCE.

SO NEXT TIME YOU READ A BOOK, SHARE YOUR THOUGHTS ON YOUR BOOK WEBSITE OF CHOICE. IT HELPS PEOPLE DISCOVER THAT AUTHOR OR THAT SERIES.

YES, SOME AUTHORS LIKE GOOD BEER, TOO; BUT REVIEWS KEEP US IN THE READERS' EYES AND MINDS.

THANKS!

WWW.TEEMORRIS.COM

Figure 11-2: Apps like *ImageQuote* can help you create original images and pull quotes from your blogpost which make for easy promotion.

Using other people's images can backfire on you, however. Sure, when you are just operating as a social media individual, you might enjoy posting Tom Hiddleston memes, but as a professional trying to keep a good online reputation, you should think twice about it.

And don't forget—as we have mentioned in earlier chapters—that stealing another's meme and slapping your website URL on it, is definitely out. Similar to when blog content is syndicated without attribution, "scraping" occurs when the origins of the content are removed and posters tag the accompanying content with their own page, giving the appearance that the shared content is their original content. Turning someone else's content into your own can come back to haunt you.

The safest thing to do when creating your own image is to stick to ones you took yourself, or you can find stock photography at sites like depositphotos.com. For a small investment, you will be on safe ground to use these photos, and if you are making your own cover, you can repurpose stock images for that, too.

Don't forget to tweak the images for different platforms. Remember tall images work great on Pinterest and Tumblr. Perfectly square ones, like Figure 11-2, work best for Instagram and Twitter.

How to Effectively Use Hashtags

We introduced the tracking tool hashtags in our Twitter chapter, and returned to hashtags when we covered Instagram, Facebook, and even Pinterest, all of these platforms taking advantage of a hashtag's trending capabilities. For authors, hashtags are best employed in the following ways:

- When developing a new title or project (#amwriting, #amediting, #WIP, #teaser)
- When working within a genre (#steampunk, #UF, #YAFantasy)
- With tweets pertaining to a book or series (#MoPO, #Redshirts)
- When identifying promotions or digital appearances (#blogtour, #podcast, #interview)
- At special events, like book festivals and conventions (#BEA2019, #balticon)

Hashtags are the best way to track discussions and trending topics from all across a social media platform; you'll even hear opinions from people you are not following. Whether you are using tracking options offered through the official Twitter app, if you review all Instagram images using a tag, or if you single-click a tag appearing in a Facebook update, hashtags allow you to follow or join in a conversation, provided participants consistently use the same hashtag in conversations and posts.

Not all posts need hashtags, but there are times, current events, and special moments when hashtags are essential.

Book events and engagements. When attending book festivals, it is always a good idea to use a hashtag for people to track you and other authors attending the event. Before arriving, try to find out if the event has an official hashtag (most events should have one as they will want metrics to show potential sponsors for the following year's event) and encourage your fellow authors and your network to use it. When creating an official hashtag, keep it easy to remember and as few characters as possible.

Topics of discussion. If you are composing updates on Instagram, or Facebook you can turn key words in your update into hashtags, making your status easily found in a hashtag search. So, if you are talking about "a new steampunk short story" you have just written, you should post the status as "a new #steampunk short story" instead. Why use steampunk as your hashtag? Steampunk is the term or topic of discussion you want people to find you under. Find those key words—no more than five, at the most—and let them work for you.

Twitter Chats. A good example of what can be done with writing chats is #scifichat. Featuring special guests, this chat covers topics of writing science fiction, fantasy, and horror. Hosted by David Rozansky @scifichat happens on Fridays. Social hour starts at 3pm EST while discussions and questions begin at 4pm EST.

When participating or simply observing in a chat, all your tweets should follow one of the hashtags used. Using the primary hashtag is enough to track with the discussion. If you are mentioning Twitter Chats on other platforms, you should use corresponding hashtags for tracking purposes.

Twitter Parties. Hosted by the author themselves or a third party, all using an agreed-upon hashtag, Twitter Parties are similar to Twitter Chats. The difference is that Twitter Parties tend to double with the use of contests:

participants (people who actively tweet or retweet content under the official hashtag) are entered into giveaways. Instead of happening on a weekly basis, these online events tend to happen before or after recent book releases, special events hosted by authors, and topics specific to the author who is hosting the Twitter Party. If you are mentioning Twitter Parties on other platforms, you should use corresponding hashtags for tracking purposes.

Similar to hashtags agreed upon by the hosts, the best hashtags are compact and easy to remember. Instead of a Twitter party hosted by #MinistryOfPeculiarOccurrences, it's hosted by #MoPO.

Accurate and consistent hashtagging of your content is good practice across a number of networks. The hashtag symbol (#) has become a way to facilitate searching and indexing on social media platforms. People who are searching for a particular topic find them useful. When a hashtag is trending, it means it is being searched a lot and used often. Hashtags do come with some simple rules. Don't string too many words together, unless it is for comedy. For example, #mybookisawesomeandyoushouldbuyit is not going to get you anywhere, but it will make fans chuckle a bit.

Hashtags need to be accurate and to sensibly describe your content. Hijacking a popular or trending topic that doesn't accurately describe what you are doing (another form of "trolling") is a terrible idea. Such tactics inevitably backfire.

How so?

When popular brand name pizza DiGiorno used the hashtag #whyIstayed (which was about women and domestic violence) to advertise their pizza, the backlash was horrible. They had to respond with "A million apologies. Did not read what the hashtag was about before posting," which, in admitting DiGiorno was oblivious to the hashtag's intent, makes a bad situation worse.

Understanding what a hashtag is referencing before posting or contributing is always a good idea. If you have no idea, or just want to be sure you're not using someone else's hashtag, then visit tagdef.com. There you can find out what certain hashtags mean, or even define your own. Just check out one we created earlier: https://tagdef.com/mopo.

However, as useful as hashtags are, you can go overboard with them and lose the message you are trying to communicate. Stick to between five to ten hashtags in one post at the most. While some third-party apps will create (no kidding) fifty or more hashtags for your posts, you take the chance of red carding your update as SPAM. Other platforms like Instagram, pictured in Figure 11-3, will limit the amount of hashtags you can use in a post so you can avoid turning your posts into SPAM.

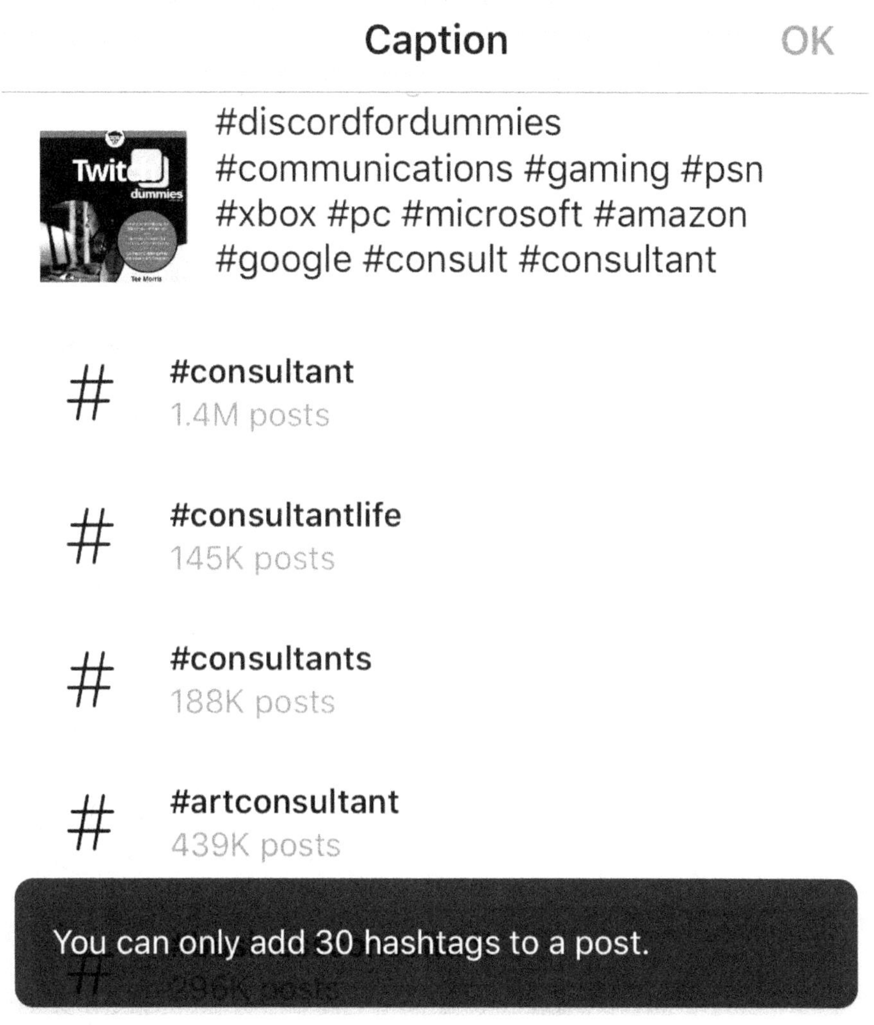

Caption   OK

#discordfordummies
#communications #gaming #psn
#xbox #pc #microsoft #amazon
#google #consult #consultant

\#   **#consultant**
     1.4M posts

\#   **#consultantlife**
     145K posts

\#   **#consultants**
     188K posts

\#   **#artconsultant**
     439K posts

You can only add 30 hashtags to a post.
\#   296K posts

Figure 11-3: Instagram, in response to some social media gurus and influencers abusing hashtags, implemented limits to how many hashtags you can use in a single post.

Here are some good writerly tags for connecting with your readers: #FridayReads #BookGiveaway #MustRead #StoryFriday #LitChat #FreeBook #Kindle #Nook, and don't forget you can also hashtag your genre (#YA). If you are looking to network with other authors, try one of the following: #AmWriting #AmEditing #WriteChat #AskAuthor #SelfPub #FridayReads

Taking P!nk's Advice: Facebook Parties

I'm comin' up so you better get this party started
Get this party started on a Saturday night
Everybody's waiting for me to arrive...

You know that sassy rock star P!nk is absolutely right—people love a party, even an online one, so it's not surprising that advertisers have picked up on the chance to rally people online for a Facebook Party. Writers can get in on the fun of these special events and create some visibility for their book titles in the process.

Before announcing your party, though, ask yourself first what you are celebrating.? No one celebrates an ordinary day of the week. They celebrate milestone events. As a writer, the biggest event of the season should be your book birthday, but you could also host an event for bundling your books together, a Kickstarter campaign for an anthology, or a cover reveal. Be careful you don't tire out your guests with too many parties in the course of one a year.

Like a party that you would throw in your off-line life, the planning of an online party is important. Here are some questions you need to ask yourself before you announce your next bash to the world.

What date? You want to find one that doesn't clash with major holidays like Black Friday, Christmas, Veteran's Day, or anything that could annoy or prevent your guests from attending. That doesn't mean that you can't plan your party around major days, for instance, two weeks before Christmas would be a great time to have a party to celebrate your holiday-themed book.

If you're doing a book release, you can decide to either build up excitement the week before the book comes out, or try and generate sales during the week after.

What time? Think about your readers, where the audience that are you are aiming for are, and time zones come into play. Our own *Ministry of Peculiar Occurrences* event was timed to be late in an evening, and ran for four hours, until midnight EST. That way our readers on the West Coast could still join in too. You are never going to be able to find an optimal time for everyone all over the world, but you can adjust it so that there is at least a chance for your international readers to find the party.

What sort of decorations? Set up your event from your author page. Under More/Event/Create Event, input the date and time, and make it look pretty with a header image. Preferably, something related to the book release you are celebrating or your brand.

What do I serve? You can't have food, but you can still have goodies to attract the guests. No one in the neighborhood is going to come unless you give them a reason, so think about things to giveaway. Be creative. Give away signed books, or items related to your book. Steampunk writers give away tea. Fairy-tale urban fantasy writers give away apple-related items for Snow White, or hair products for Rapunzel. Romance writers give away jewelry. Think about your book, its theme, and what your target market of readers is. Keep it fun!

Who do you invite? Guests are important, but author guests can bring a crowd. If you are just starting off in the author space (think of it as being new to your neighborhood), then you might not have met many fellow writers. Obviously if you've been to a few conventions, made contacts online, or have a writers' group, you are starting off with an advantage— if you want to include author guests. That doesn't mean you can't invite people if you're new, just be aware a relative stranger asking is not the same as someone guests feel a connection with. However, politely asking people in a similar genre who are also starting off can't hurt; bear in mind you are also offering them a way to promote their own books.

Once author guests have said yes, find a good time for them to be on. You'll want ten- to fifteen-minute slots for guests to promote and interact, but also allow some buffer time between for you to circulate and talk about your work.

The Big Night: Party Time!

As the date of the event approaches, there is still some work to do to make sure your event goes off with a bang.

Promotion. Spread the word, not just on Facebook, but on all your social media networks. Reach out to your author guests to help get the word out, and make sure you give them enough time to do so. Promotion should be around two weeks to a month out—any further out risks people forgetting, but if you promote too close to the event, then people can't plan to be there at your party. The more the merrier, after all.

Preparation. Before the event, make sure you have your timetable sorted out, but also some prepared activities and information to keep the party flowing. For your author guests, make sure you have introductions ready to go. Be personable and welcoming. For the interludes where you plan to talk, have some prepared quotes from the books, questions, and best of all images. That way if things should start to flag or go quiet, you are only a cut and paste away from keeping people entertained.

Kick Off. When the night begins, you might want to make sure you are comfortable with virtual refreshments (or real ones) at hand, because a good Facebook party can fly by. Stay close to your computer or tablet, make sure you are there to answer questions, welcome people who arrive, and keep the conversation flowing.

Limber up your fingers, too, as you will be typing fast and hard. Hey, no one ever said being a host was easy!

Having chosen what the prizes are for the party, you can run contests in several ways: randomly picking people in the party room, perhaps quizzing questions based on your book (or something related, if it isn't out yet), or rewarding the guest who comes up with the best casting of your book's dream movie. Keep your questions and trivia simple, though. Nothing is more awkward than a competition where no one wins!

The End. Don't forget to say "thank you" to your guests and author guests. Before the party is over, remind people of the essential information: where to find your book, relevant dates and times concerning its release, and your website location, so if they have more questions, they know how to find you.

Planning Makes Perfect: Before That Social Media Event

Before attending Facebook or Twitter Parties, or appearing as a "featured guest" at these events, have on hand pre-crafted posts. Concentrate on questions or topics that might get the conversation started again; and if tweets allow for space, have images ready to upload. Anticipate some of the questions readers might ask you:

- If your book was made into a movie who would play ____?
- Where do you get your inspiration?
- Who are your favorite authors?
- Why do you write (your genre)?

Make certain you publicize when and where special online events will be taking place. Publicize your Chats and Parties across your blog, your podcast, and other platforms. People do not randomly appear for these events—they wait to hear from you.

Finally, especially if you are the special guest or are hosting a social media event, make certain you have all you need at arm's length. Have a drink close by. Make sure you've gone to the bathroom before go time. Once the event starts, don't leave your chair. The conversation will fly fast and furious.

Attribution, Not Imitation, Is the Sincerest Form of Flattery

Being a good participant in social media means sometimes going the extra mile. If you do end up reposting pictures of cosplay (where people dress up as their favorite comic book, video game, or book characters), or someone else's travel adventures, retain any attribution the image came with. People who create things—and authors are part of that tribe—like to be credited for their work.

If there is an awesome image you really want to post, but it has been stripped of attribution, then you can go the extra mile. Put on your deerstalker hat and seek out the missing information.

It's actually easier than you think. Go to https://tineye.com/ and upload or paste a link to the image. On clicking the Search button, TinEye will do its best to help you find the original owner. It may seem like a bother, but it's the way you will cultivate a professional image. The same goes for memes and motivationals—check the source. No one likes to have a reader point out that "Einstein did not actually say that."

If this kind of research seems like too much, just stick to posting links and images you have purchased or made yourself.

Seek Out Your Audience

Every book has an audience, a market you are aiming for, but it won't come beating on your door. The truth is you have to find out where your people are, and go to them. Think about yourself and your book, where do you best fit?

If you still don't have an idea, look at where authors in your genre are concentrating. Do they appear to be having success on these platforms? Start building your community of readers in those places.

Have a Plan

The leading cause of failure in social media is when people jump into platforms without any idea what to do. Social media is not something you do because "everyone else is doing it." You do it because you have something to accomplish.

When you set up a blog, ask yourself how often you intend to blog. Will you be using Facebook to promote your blog? How often will you post on Facebook or Twitter? Will you go beyond these three sites and work with Tumblr? Instagram? Podcasting? What will your voice be? Will you be all business, or will you pepper in personal thoughts? The more you map out your plan, the more focused your online platform will be.

These tips provide a great foundation for social media initiatives. Applying them to your networks can make your platform easier to develop and build, and make your signal strong and reliable. When you use social media to its full potential, you are actually building and developing your brand. Social media can help to define your brand.

The scary thing about brands, though, is that they are fragile and easily damaged. As important as it is to know what to do in social media, it is equally important to know what not to do. When you have the right strategy, most, if not all, of the missteps made in social media can easily be avoided.

Focus on Maintaining a Signal, Not Creating Noise

When talking about social media and social networking, you may hear the term Signal-to-Noise Ratio. Signal-to-Noise refers to the quality of your statuses and updates. If you are constantly advertising or promoting something in your feed, your audience may tune out your updates and so they are considered "noise." Updates that your audience genuinely cares about or interacts with are referred to as your "signal." When it comes to social media, it is easy to slip into noise mode. Signal is all about quality and what you deliver to your network.

So how do you avoid becoming that author?

Make a connection with your fan base through articles that capture the imagination. Share what you do when you are not writing. Do you have a passion for classical theater, B movies, or fashion? Tap into one of those topics. Post images, video, and your own blog articles on what it is that captures your attention or helps you unwind. Post this kind of content alongside interesting news articles rooted in your genre. On your fifth post, go ahead and post a quick promotion for your book. When a new review appears for it, share it on Facebook and Twitter. Celebrate with the community. You want to aim for a ratio of one promotional post to every five, or three promos out of every ten. People who follow you on networks will know that while you are there to promote your book, you are not there to do only that. You're a real person with real interests and passions outside of writing.

Figure 11-4: When it comes to improving the signal over the noise, Pip and Tee focus less on "their latest releases" and more on the writer's lifestyle on *The Shared Desk*. Sure, they do talk about their latest releases when they happen; but the podcast goes well beyond their own promotions.

These are all practices that we have seen writers carry out across networks, many of them finding success in creating strong street teams (fans who love to talk to others about your books and who help you make the sale) for their works currently on the bookshelves or coming soon to bookstores everywhere. Sadly, though, the success stories of social media are not what drove us to write this book. This particular social media guide is born out of our frustration, anger, and outright wonder with authors who get online and make a mess of things. Our inspiration comes from the writers who don't know when to quit pitching their books, when to walk away from an argument, and when not to say a damn thing.

To the overly aggressive author on the Internet, this next section's for you.

Anti-Social Media: What to Avoid in Online Promotion and Networking

There are a lot of things that you can get right in social media, but it is easy to get things wrong if you don't know what you are doing. Even if you do know what you are doing, you can still make mistakes. There's a difference between stumbling (which you can easily recover from) and hitting the ground hard, face first.

Forgetting the "Social" Aspect of Social Media

Many writers in social media tend to accept the bad advice of gurus who say that every tweet, Facebook blog post, and post on Tumblr should be an advertisement for their next book. The other bad advice is to make your feed a fountain of evergreen content—retweets or inspiring quotes, like Figure 11-5, and then ads for your books. It is not uncommon to see this, and this is not how you build a platform or broaden a network. This is merely adding noise to your signal (as we defined earlier), so much noise that your followers will essentially tune you out. Keep your promotional posts under control. They should not become the sole voice and purpose of your social platforms.

Figure 11-5: Redundant content with little-to-no engagement does nothing to build your brand or establish connections with others in your network.

Another rule of thumb in social media is to establish yourself as an individual and to invest time in building your network. The key is to do so in a smart and diplomatic manner. The best way to break this rule is to make your first communication on Twitter a DM that encourages others to join your Facebook Page.

Social media is about you, but it should not all be about you.

Scraping: The Fastest Way to Get Yourself Kicked Out of the Pool

Yes, we are going to talk about scraping again. Why? Because it happens so frequently and because it's so bad for your professional reputation.

The lure of the Dark Side is strong. Maybe you have one week when you simply feel like you have nothing interesting to say. But, hey, that wacky Chuck Wendig wrote a brilliant post on most frequently asked writing questions. It's out there on the Internet, so it's fair game. You might be thinking, *I comment on Chuck's blog, so we're pals. He won't mind. I'll just cut and paste the post into my blog post and...*

NO!

Seriously—scraping will give you a bad name and make enemies in the writing world. Scraping should, however, not be confused with its kinder, more community-minded cousin, syndication. Scraping involves taking the whole post and dropping it into your page complete.

Here's a word that's synonymous with scraping: *plagiarism.* That is what scraping is, essentially.

You might even mention the original author's name or include his link, but that is not a pass in this instance. You have just stolen content, and eyeballs, from the creator of that content. The link back is worthless, since viewers just got all the good juice from your page. Remember that syndication occurs when a portion of the blog post (the first paragraph, or two, at the most) is pasted with proper attribution and the link back to the original blogger. That makes for happy content creators. Scraping will get you a bad reputation, and no invitations to their next birthday party.

And if you think authors and content creators don't notice these things . . . well, you're wrong there, too.

Friends at Wholesale: The Perils of Purchasing Likes or Followers

Many social media gurus encourage "investing" into your platforms, usually followed by the *"I can help you triple your Twitter followers for the low, low price of ... "*

Incredibly large numbers on platforms do look impressive, but a large price comes for tens of thousands of Likes on Facebook and nameless, faceless Followers on Twitter. Purchased Likes originate from Like Farms, companies that pay their employees to "Like" hundreds upon hundreds of pages, tweets, and posts of various products, personalities, and services featured on social networks. These Like Farms fill your statistics with numbers, but do not take any active role or interaction with your community. While you suddenly appear to have those "rock star" statistics, these inflated numbers burn through your advertising budget and cost you more when it comes time to boost posts. On other platforms, these bulk Followers are nothing more than automated "bots" that tweet nonsense, junking up your incoming tweets and making it harder and harder for you to track your main Twitter feed. Other popular Twitter accounts purchased in bulk include pornography sources and malware carriers. Follower Purchases on Instagram will spam your feed with a sudden dumping of images, many of them random, innocuous posts of what it is they are selling, turning your Instagram feed into a Sears catalog.

Not only do these accounts distance you from your network, limiting you to interact with those who directly mention you, but they can damage your online brand as these bots will find unsuspecting targets from your own networks. Be wary with these paid services, as they lead to nothing but noise.

Message Garbled, Say Again: Avoid Nonsense in Your Feed

Inspirational quotes. Retweets. Promotions of your latest book.

If these are occasionally in your feed, that's one thing. If any of these are your feed, you are missing the point of Twitter. Or Instagram. Or Tumblr.

People follow you on social networks to find out more about you, not about who you follow or what other people have said. Whether you are filling your Instagram with an endless parade of products or simply having your Facebook echo your Twitter account, make your content original and understandable.

A Garden Gone to Seed: The Danger of Unattended and Abandoned Accounts

From his time in the Information Security field, Tee can tell you from experience that many InfoSec professionals are opposed to many of the networks covered in this book, as security tends to be overlooked when these services are developed and brought online. The vulnerabilities present in Facebook, Tumblr, and other social media platforms are a genuine concern as social networks are easily commandeered by hackers, especially when accounts are left unattended and underutilized. Keep your account active with daily postings, and watch for any odd activity or suspicious postings appearing under your name. If you find that a platform is not for you, it is best to delete the account completely rather than to leave it live. Lack of activity on any social media platform opens your brand to damage.

There is another method hackers use to gain control of social media contacts. It is a method of infiltration called "social engineering." You see this most often in e-mails from PayPal and banks informing you that your account will be shut down in twenty-four hours if you do not visit a link provided in the e-mail. On Facebook and Twitter, social engineering most commonly happens in direct messaging. Usually the messages will say something along the lines of *"LOL Have u seen this vid?"* followed by a link, or something similar to what's pictured in Figure 11-6. On rare occasions, these messages appear from accounts you recognize (possibly someone who has been hacked), but they mostly come from strangers (bots). Anytime you receive messages that appear to be sent by people who don't have time to spell out words, chances are the account has been compromised. Contact that user (on a public channel) and inform them (politely) that you received a direct message that you were uncertain of.

Figure 11-6: Whenever accounts are left unattended or breached by hackers, members of the network are systematically contacted with random links. These links can lead to bad actors of cybersecurity.

Come on Feel the Noise: Oversharing

When it comes to sharing, you must decide where you draw the line in what you will share and what you won't. Social media is your platform for your works and for you as an author. It is not your therapist's couch. Oversharing, that sudden outpour of emotion and in-your-face position-taking, can not only alienate your online network of contacts, both personal and professional, but can also reflect poorly on you.

Oversharing is nothing new in social networking, but it is far too easy a trap to fall into. Do you want to become known as "that guy" or "that girl?" To help prevent taking a misstep, the first and foremost question to ask yourself every single time you are ready to post is: "Should I be sharing this?" It would be great to say that people think before they post, but sadly some are more about sending out a snappy, witty update or sharing with the world than considering who's watching their feeds.

This chapter offers you a good look at a simple and sound approach to Content Marketing. You are now working with social media on a higher level than the casual user. You're thinking of online networking as a strategic exercise, as a platform to promote your works and develop a brand for yourself. We've also offered an honest look about how Content Marketing can take a wrong turn. Many of these problems are easily course corrected, provided you can recognize what doesn't work in those ill-advised approaches.

However, what happens when things go completely wrong? What we refer to is not when the content, but the content creator, takes a direction that could have been easily avoided. Far too often, writers makes choices that baffle and befuddle the world, often causing heads to cock one side and invoke the question "What were you thinking?" Crisis Management is something you may not want to think about, but it should be part of your social media plan. This is how we're wrapping up this comprehensive look at social media: It is never a bad idea to think through what might happen when online activity gets completely out of control.

XII: SOCIAL MEDIA SECURITY

THE BEST WAY TO MANAGE A PROBLEM IN SOCIAL MEDIA IS TO AVOID IT

Throughout this book, you have gotten a look at social media from a hard, strategic approach as opposed to *"Hey, all the cool kids are doing this — LET'S JUMP ON IN!!!"* A lot of the wild abandon you see writers, artists, content creators, and larger entities on the corporate level approach social media with is due in part to the spontaneous whimsy that these platforms engender. Just in the names alone you see it . . .

Twitter.

Snapchat.

YouTube.

Untappd.

Social media tends to be easily dismissed, even today. It's thought of as a cesspool of the worst people, or a distraction from what really matters: writing. Perhaps the biggest problem with social media is this strange belief that anybody can do it, when in reality social media is that it isn't all that simple. If social media comes easy to you, then it means that you're comfortable with it. That's a major advantage. Another advantage is having a plan. Without vision or direction, social media—and all the sequential communications around it—is a rudderless boat with a broken wheel on the bridge. So yes, you should have a plan for when things go well.

You should also have a plan when things go horribly wrong.

Anti-Social Media: The Sequel

There are a lot of things that you can get right in social media, but it is easy to get things wrong if you don't know what you are doing. Even if you do know what you are doing, you can still make mistakes. There's a difference between stumbling (which you can easily recover from) and hitting the ground hard, face first.

Many writers in social media tend to accept the bad advice of gurus who say that every tweet, Facebook blog post, and post on Tumblr should be an advertisement for their next book. It is not uncommon to see authors adding noise to social media, so much so that followers will essentially tune them out. Promotional posts should not become the sole voice and purpose of your social platforms.

Neither should your social media platforms be a circular promotion for yourself. This is what happens when your first communication on one platform is a post encouraging people to join your other networks.

No. Just…no.

There is nothing wrong with giving people a list of other locations where you can be found. (Quick tip: Use a pinned tweet to let people know your other social links or create a Nightbot command that will let people know while you are streaming content where your other social links are.) Should a post promoting something—your books or social networks—be your first post? No. It should be a greeting. It should be a sincere invitation to join the conversation. When building platforms and networks, establish yourself as an individual and invest time in building your network through a dialog.

One final thought concerning inspirational quotes and retweets: If these are occasionally in your feed, that's one thing. If inspirational quotes, retweets, and your book promotions are your feed, you are missing the point of social media. People follow you on social networks to find out more about you, not about who you follow or what other people have said. Make your content original and engaging.

First impressions are everything, so think about what that initial contact and your feed says about you.

Focusing on the *Quality*, not the *Quantity*: The Statistics Game

You will be told time and time again how important it is to have the big numbers on your platforms, but ask, "Exactly how do you interact with 100,000 people?"

You don't. You can announce something, but with those numbers it isn't always about interaction. It can be disheartening when you only have a few thousand, or a few hundred people on your Facebook page, or your Instagram account. So, remind yourself you are trying to build a community.

Then understand this, many of those huge numbers you see on other accounts, are not in fact real people. Many are bound to be purchased and originate from Like Farms where companies pay employees to "Like" hundreds upon hundreds of pages of various products, personalities, and services featured on social networks. For a few dollars, many users hike their follower numbers.

While, these Like Farms fill your statistics with numbers, they do not take any active role or interaction with your community. While you suddenly appear to have those "rock star" statistics, these inflated numbers burn through your advertising budget and cost you more when it comes time to boost posts. Not only do these accounts distance you from your network, limiting you to interact with those who directly mention you, but they can damage your online brand as these bots will find unsuspecting targets from your own networks. Be wary with these paid services, as they lead to nothing but noise.

Big numbers on platforms do look impressive, but it comes at a price. Check those people who are requesting to follow you on networks. When a user starts to follow you on Instagram, for instance, it is always a good idea to check the account to see if it is an actual person with a story or a product to sell. Look at the accounts, evaluate the feed, and see if this is someone you want to connect with.

Content Marketing FAIL: When a Strategy Turns South

Content marketing, as covered earlier in this book, can be a positive, community-building strategy for any individual or business, be it a writer, a publisher, or even a literary agency. However, some writers and social media mavericks use the concept of content marketing as an umbrella for shady strategies. One unethical approach to sharing content through photo tagging.

If you are unfamiliar with it, this feature occurs when you upload a photograph or video and use the "Tag Photo" (a common option on social platforms) where you can identify someone in the photo. The result can be a live link created to your account, an image on your Timeline, or a notification that you've been mentioned.

To be clear: a random picture that has nothing to do with an event you attended, or anything remotely related to you appears on your Timeline, openly promoting another author's book. You have the option of removing your tag from the innocuous image but remember that some authors will exercise the right to tag you in the image again.

And this has happened to us. Repeatedly.

If you are tagging other authors in photos, be sure that they depict something relevant. By relevant, we mean an appearance at which the author is seen in the picture, the cover of an anthology where their work appears, or something that you know will appeal to their tastes. Tagging photos to specifically promote yourself is nothing less than SPAM.

Finally, there is the content marketing strategy that is less about branding and more about the rope-a-dope approach to marketing. If you are unfamiliar with the term, rope-a-dope is a boxing strategy where Opponent A feigns exhaustion by leaning into the ropes of the ring. Opponent B goes on the offensive, unaware that Opponent A is in a defensive position, allowing the ropes and his arms taking the shock of the blows. When Opponent B begins to show fatigue, Opponent A goes on the offensive. How this works in bad content marketing: We were followed by a writer, or at least this individual identified themselves as a writer and reader of books, and their feed featured several books and selfies in their office. Five posts, so a relatively new account. From the point of returning a follow on several platforms, the tone of the account changed from "my adventures in writing" to five posts a day featuring make-up tutorials, the accompanying posts going into detail on specific brands used in said tutorial.

How is this different from branding? In Tee's feed, he features five posts about writing or streaming content; but then he will also feature whatever new Funko Pop figurine he's purchased. The brand in this case — Tee is a writer and content creator who takes his Funko Pops seriously. (And he does.) If the postings are flipped, and Tee's writing posts are one or two against his ten Funko Pop postings — and let's say four of those posts happen in one day — this account is no longer about your brand but about promoting a product.

Taking a Stand: When Authors Express Themselves

If you look at the history of social media and writers, it seems to be a monthly occurrence where something goes completely pear-shaped. and then a tsunami of responses begins to form. It can be about headlines from the press. It can be about socially charged issues. It can be about something that you believe to your core to be right or wrong. Or it could be doubling down on a bad review or someone's opinion on your work. This is where social media management is paramount. Whatever your passion, you share your thoughts on social media which is your right. There is nothing wrong with expressing yourself, even if it is outside the realm and scope of your books.

Just remember, people can—and will—disagree with you. If you want to speak your mind, nothing will stop you. However, depending on the subject matter, there may be fallout. If you want to take a stand, do so; but depending on what that stand is, don't expect all of your readers to fall in line. Some may push back. You have to do the calculations for your own career. How important is this issue, and are you OK with the consequences that might come from it? If people stop buying your books, is it still worth it?

These decisions are highly personal, and everyone has their own line in the sand. All we recommend is before you post something about a hot button issue, take more than a second to think about it.

 Before invoking your First Amendment right to express yourself, let's take a look at the amendment:

Congress shall make no law respecting an establishment of religion, or prohibiting the free exercise thereof; or abridging the freedom of speech, or of the press; or the right of the people peaceably to assemble, and to petition the government for a redress of grievances.

Feel free to read it again. This amendment reads that the *government* cannot prohibit you from speaking your mind. Nowhere does it say the *general public* cannot react to your First Amendment right.
You certainly have the right to say whatever you want. You also have the right to deal with the consequences of saying whatever you want.

If only people thought before they posted, but sadly some are more about sending out a snappy, witty comeback or edgy epiphany that hit you while you were in the shower. If a post does invoke a reaction you didn't expect or want, an initial reaction is to take the post down. Sure, you can do that; but screen capturing is not only easy to do, it is commonplace. (Consider that most of the artwork featured in this book is all screen caps.) Once live, a post simply doesn't "go away" just because you deleted it. You have made your thoughts on a matter known and you put them out on the Internet. This is the genie free of the bottle with little chance of stuffing it back in with the use of the Delete button.

Authors tend to get themselves into trouble:

- Responding to negative reviews.
- Responding to inaccurate or incorrect opinions on their works.
- Responding to something "misinterpreted" or "misquoted" in an interview, blogpost, or article.
- Responding or expressing socially charged opinions.

Yes, if you want to step into these kinds of conversations, no one will stop you. Not even us. However, what will you gain from any of these confrontations? The last word? That's rare. Whether the posters are just trolls or impassioned book critics, they have chosen this hill to be the one they will die on. "Till the end of the line," as Cap would say to Bucky. If you're looking at this as some form of brand management, consider that the offending post is fishing for a bite. Particularly with trolls, it's all about the reaction which can spawn another reaction, and so on. You do need to ask yourself before undertaking a discussion like this if it is worth the argument.

The Art of Owning It: When You Say Something Wrong

The fact that you have a by-line does not make you perfect, omnipotent, or precognitive. You may believe that you are in the right, innocent of wrong-doing, or far more "woke" than those around you; but then some undeniable fact—a clear contradiction to your statement—is brought to the foreground. While it is never pleasant to be wrong, it can (and will) happen.

So, if a well-intended post completely backfires, your reaction should be a simple one: *own it.*

There's nothing wrong in being wrong. You're human, and we're flawed creatures. What says a lot about you is how you own it (a/k/a apologize) when you discover "I still have something to learn about this subject matter." And it says a lot about how you as a professional handle a moment when you are wrong.

Some phrases to avoid when owning it:

- "Well, actually . . ."
- "To be fair . . ." / "TBF . . ."
- "I apologize, but you have to understand . . ."
- "I apologize, but I was provoked . . ."
- "I'm sorry you aren't smart enough to recognize . . ."

You've made a mistake. Apologize sincerely, and then take steps to make sure this doesn't happen again. Grow from your mistakes. That is a challenge in the wake of any mistake you make. The authors of this book have built social media platforms that remain reliable and trustworthy to those who visit. That does not mean Tee and Pip are perfect in their execution, or that they think they are perfect. The authors of this title have managed to avoid "shooting from the hip" (so far!) where many mistakes come from. That doesn't mean they haven't typed out a fired-up response or reaction to an unverified headline. They just didn't click that all-powerful "Post" or "Update" button.

Take a moment to check and double-check yourself before posting. And if you make a mistake, own it.

History Has Its Eyes on You: Authors Behaving Badly

In our chapter on unconventional platforms for social media, we cover Untappd, Vivino, and Distiller, or what we call the "social" social apps. We mentioned legendary writers who enjoyed a good drink or several, but it's worthwhile to note some authors have been known to love their drink a little too much. Authors may joke about "BarCon" and how they can party like rock stars; but speaking as a couple who enjoy the occasional cocktail, moderation should be first and foremost. As you're checking in your happy hour libations, make sure you're not socializing to a point of where you lose control of your manners, or worse—blackout. Maybe it sounds like we're preaching here, but to be blunt everyone now has a camera within reach and love to post photos on social media. Make sure photos posted of you are not photos you will regret.

And also keep in mind that not everyone enjoys a good scotch, wine, or beer, or simply don't drink at all. Don't make a big deal if someone chooses an iced tea not from Long Island. Respect your fellow authors' choices, and enjoy the social time, online or offline regardless.

Regardless of whether or not alcohol is involved, you should keep in mind that cameras are everywhere now. Tee's first instructor in martial arts told him "The best way to avoid a punch is not to be there when it happens," and that can easily be said about avoiding potentially embarrassing or character damaging situations. Sometimes, you don't see them coming, but if you look around and ask yourself "Could this be a problem for me?" then chances are it is. Listen to that instinct of yours which might be a bit smarter in the moment than you.

Crisis management in social media is not difficult but there is also no cut-and-dry approach either. Each situation is unique. It can be equally frustrating, exhausting, and taxing in trying to manage a problematic situation online. Sometimes, problems can be disarmed with a simple, sincere apology. On the other end of the spectrum, authors can be subject to intense cyberbullying against you and your family. That's a wide spectrum to cover, we know; but the best advice in crisis management in social media comes from Science Fiction legend, Douglas Adams: Don't panic. There are plenty of options you have to assist in your management through a crisis, provided you keep a cool head and stick to a plan. There is no guarantee you will ever need to consult this chapter on what to do. Just be smart before going social. That may sound like common knowledge we're sharing here, but when you watch other authors embracing the spontaneity of social media, you might discover that this knowledge is more uncommon than you might expect.

Social networking has become a way that we communicate with people, both one-on-one and around the world; but there are limits. To sharing. To connecting. To communicating. These limits are set by you. Social media platforms serve as fantastic outlets, so long as you approach them responsibly and reasonably. Remember that your brand is at stake, your reputation, and therefore your activity using social media warrants your full attention. Social networking is an investment in your career and should be cared for and cultivated. Go beyond networking and build a community around your work. This community can become your street team for future book releases and events you will be attending, increasing your profile both in the online world and the real one.

Good luck and good hunting!

photo by Bruce F. Press Photography

New Zealand-born fantasy writer and podcaster **Philippa (Pip) Ballantine** is the author of the *Books of the Order* series, and has appeared in collections such as *Steampunk World* and *Clockwork Fairy Tales*. She is also the co-author with her husband, **Tee Morris,** of *The Ministry of Peculiar Occurrences* series. Both the series and its companion podcast, *Tales from the Archives,* have won numerous awards including the 2011 Airship Award for Best in Steampunk Literature, the 2013 Parsec Award for Best Podcast Anthology, and RT Reviewers' Choice for Best Steampunk of 2014.

Tee penned *Twitch for Dummies* and *Discord for Dummies*, co-authored *Podcasting for Dummies,* and has spoken on streaming media, social media, and other tech-related topics across the country and around the world, including such places as the Library of Congress, Te Papa Tongarewa, AwesomeCon, and MAGFest. He has also contributed articles and stories for numerous anthologies including *Farscape Forever!, Tales of a Tesla Ranger,* and *A Cosmic Christmas 2 You.*

The two reside in Manassas, Virginia with their daughter and a mighty clowder of cats. You can find out more about them at **pjballantine.com, teemorris.com,** or **twitch.tv/theteemonster.**